This book was set in Palatino by Windfall Software using ZzTEX and was printed and bound in the United States of America.

Library of Congress Cataloging-in-Publication Data

Perry, John, 1943–
  Knowledge, possibility, and consciousness / John Perry.
    p. cm. — (The Jean Nicod lectures ; 1999)
  Includes bibliographical references and index.
  ISBN 0-262-16199-0 (alk. paper)
  1. Knowledge, Theory of. I. Title. II. Series.
BD161 .P43   2001
128'.2—dc21   00-048959

To the memory of my brother
Tom Perry
1941–1998

Contents

Contents

Series Foreword

The Jean Nicod Lectures are delivered annually in Paris by a leading philosopher of mind or philosophically oriented cognitive scientist. The 1993 inaugural lectures marked the centenary of the birth of the French philosopher and logician Jean Nicod (1893–1931). The lectures are sponsored by the Centre National de la Recherche Scientifique (CNRS) as part of its effort to develop the interdisciplinary field of cognitive science in France. The series hosts the texts of the lectures or the monographs they inspire.

Jacques Bouveresse, President of the Jean Nicod Committee
André Holley, Director of the Cognitive Science Program, CNRS
François Recanati, Secretary of the Jean Nicod Committee and Editor of the Series

Jean Nicod Committee

Mario Borillo

Jean-Pierre Changeux

Jean-Gabriel Ganascia

Michel Imbert

Peirre Jacob

Jacques Mehler

Philippe de Rouilhan

Dan Sperber

Preface

This book is based on the Nicod lectures given in Lyon and Paris in June 1999. I am very thankful to the Centre National de la Recherche Scientifique (CNRS) and the Nicod Lecture Committee for selecting me, and to Jacques Bouveresse, André Holley, Pierre Jacob, François Recanati, Daniel Andler, Joëlle Proust, Jerome Dokic, Jerome Pelletier, and other French philosophers and cognitive scientists for the hospitality they showed me. The Centre de Recherche en Epistémologie Appliquée (CREA) and Maison Suger were fine hosts.

The central ideas of this book were presented earlier at the Chapel Hill Philosophy Colloquium in 1998 and at colloquia at various universities. They have been shaped over many years, with many influences, for better or worse. I remember being interested in the problems discussed in this book while I was an undergraduate at Doane College. I had a job delivering appliances throughout a wide area of southeastern Nebraska, and as I drove the Wanek's Furniture truck across the countryside I tried to keep my mind on Wittgenstein's arguments about beetles and boxes. I had the feeling that if I was bright enough, and tried hard enough, the troublesome beetle in my box would be revealed as a bit of conceptual confusion and disappear. Thank goodness it never

did. Laurence Nemirow rekindled my interest in these problems when I had the good luck to work with him on his
dissertation at Stanford in the late 1970s. Although in chapter 7 I disagree with part of Nemirow's analysis, his ideas
and particularly the emphasis he put on the role of imagination in our concepts of sensory states greatly influenced
me. Many years later, Güven Güzeldere came to Stanford
and raised everyone's consciousness about consciousness.
My Nicod lectures, like Fred Dretske's before them, owed
a great deal to Güzeldere. In particular Güzeldere encour-
aged me to give a talk at an American Philosophical Association symposium on my first rather inchoate ideas about
how work on indexicals and reflexivity might be relevant to
the knowledge argument. We discussed all aspects of the argument and qualia at great length while he worked on his
dissertation at Stanford. He was a superb student and a superb teacher. At about the same time Güven was at Stanford,
Lydia Sanchez was working on her dissertation, which emphasized issues related to the subject matter doctrine and
problems of unreflected identity. Talking these issues over
with Lydia was very helpful

After the first draft of this book was completed, I received
helpful comments from a number of philosophers, including Güzeldere, Ned Block, Eros Corazza, Chuck Marks, John
Fischer, Carlo Penco, David Barnett, Matthew Barrett, and
Tim Schroeder. Robert C. Jones made a very clear and persuasive presentation of the draft to the Pat Suppes–Dagfinn
Follesdal seminar on consciousness at Stanford. I had the
wonderful opportunity to attend the Ned Block–Tom Nagel
seminar at New York University during a session on the
draft of my book. Listening to Nagel and Block disagree
about what I should have said or meant was particularly
instructive. These comments and interactions led to a new
version of the last chapter and a number of changes in ear-

lier chapters. Matthew Barrett's comments convinced me I ought to have more to say than I do about the problem of other minds, especially the minds Martians might have. But I haven't yet figured out what to say, except that I can't see that neo-dualism would help. Parts of the draft were used in my freshman seminars on consciousness; the students' reactions and comments were quite helpful. Rebecca Talbott kept me from making a serious error in chapter 5.

The Nicod lectures and the final rewrite of the book were both completed in Bonn, Germany, where I spent the spring quarters of 1999 and 2000. This was made possible by a prize from the Humboldt Foundation. These stays were rewarding and productive thanks to the hospitality of Ranier Stuhlmann-Laeisz and the other members of the Insitute für Logic und Grundlagenforschung at the University of Bonn; I especially thank Albert Newen for his support and friendship.

I owe a considerable debt to the philosophers I discuss in this book. Giving a seminar on David Chalmers' exciting and absorbing book, *The Conscious Mind*, was especially helpful; it is full of ideas and arguments that clarified a number of things for me, even while I continued to disagree with the central thesis. A number of authors whom I do not discuss—David Rosenthal, John Searle, Daniel Dennett, and Patricia Churchland, to mention just four who represent a broad spectrum of approaches—have also influenced my ideas a great deal, even though I don't fully understand at this point how all of the insights can be fit together.

I am dedicating this book to my late brother Tom. We loved to discuss and argue about all sorts of things, including philosophy. Tom was full of interesting ideas and was imaginative and passionate about all sorts of issues. He wrote and enjoyed science fiction, and I suspect he thought philosophy was basically a way of thinking about the same issues without having nearly so much fun. Writing science fiction was a hobby on which he hoped to focus when he retired, but sadly cancer cut that dream short. He spent most of his career with IBM, first as a technical writer, then as a computer scientist, working on a variety of platforms from the 1960s into the 1990s. I'm sure that some of his ideas and inventions are at work inside my computer as I write this.

When we were both in our early teenage years Tom came up with the theory that there was only one soul in the universe, which traveled backward in time each time a person died and was recycled as some other person's soul. That was the first time I tried hard to think of reasons against a philosophical theory. I didn't come up with any objections that he couldn't shoot down. Finally he convinced me this was the most minimal and economical form of dualism, a perfect example of Occam's Razor. We had a lot of fun figuring out how this theory would work. So Tom was the first to bring up the challenge of dualism, not to mention personal identity. As I've mentioned elsewhere, Tom, who was a couple of years older, once told me he would "give me ten dollars tomorrow." This repeated promise amused him for a couple of days and gave rise to my interest in indexicality.

I don't suppose Tom stuck with his one-soul theory, but he certainly would have sided with Leibniz, Ewing, Chalmers, Jackson, and Kripke on the issues I discuss in this book. He thought physicalism was pretty dumb. As a computer scientist, he was particularly scornful of theories that held that the human mind was anything like a computer. It's somewhat odd to dedicate my defense of physicalism to him, but these are the only views I have to offer.

1   Experience and Neo-Dualism

. . . the terms "subjective" and "private" . . . in one of their commonly proper and serviceable usages are not to be considered as logically incompatible with "objective" or "public." . . . Private states in this philosophically quite innocuous sense are then simply central *states.*

—Herbert Feigl, *The "Mental" and The "Physical": The Essay and a Postscript*

One way to explain my goal in this little book is to say that I am trying to defend the philosophical coherence of the 1966 Academy Award winning movie *Fantastic Voyage* (Fleischer 1966). In this movie, a very important person has a brain clot, and since it would be a disaster if this person's brain were damaged in any way, because he knows something very important, the government decides to shrink a team of neurosurgeons until they are extremely small, put them in a very tiny submarine, and inject them into the bloodstream of the very important person. They make their way to the blood clot, destroy it with their miniature laser guns, and, after many adventures, including the destruction of their submarine, wade their way to safety, leaving the body through a tear duct. It is not the philosophical coherence of the main plot of the movie that I wish to defend. It is simply one remark that a member of the rescue team makes while they are mid-brain. A sort of beautiful blue vapor arises from a certain part of the brain, capturing the attention of the rescuers. Awestruck, Arthur Kennedy says to Raquel Welch, "Look, we are the first to actually see human thoughts," or words to that effect. No one in the boat finds this the least bit odd.

1.1 The Experience Gap Argument

The episode in *Fantastic Voyage* assumes that it is conceivable that one might observe, using one's physical senses, a thought or experience of another. This is a natural view to have, if one thinks, as I do, that our thoughts and experiences are events in our brains. A long and a quite distinguished philosophical tradition finds this view preposterous. Leibniz invited us to imagine that the brain was enlarged to the size of a flour mill, so we could walk inside and see all that was happening. It is obvious, he said, that we would not see anything like a thought or experience (Leibniz 1714). A couple of centuries later, British philosopher A. C. Ewing put the point like this:

Nineteenth-century materialists were . . . inclined to identify thinking, and mental events generally, with processes in the central nervous system or brain. In order to refute such views I shall suggest your trying an experiment. Heat a piece of iron red-hot, then put your hand on it, and note carefully what you feel. You will have no difficulty in observing that it is quite different from anything which a physiologist could observe, [when] he considered your . . . brain processes. The throb of pain experienced will not be . . . like anything described in textbooks of physiology as happening in the nervous system or brain. I do not say that it does not happen in the brain, but it is quite distinct from anything that other people could observe if they looked into your brain. . . . We know by experience

what feeling pain is like and we know by experience what the physiological reactions to it are, and the two are totally unlike . . . the
difference is as plainly marked and as much an empirical matter as
that between a sight and a sound. The physiological and the mental
characteristics may conceivably belong to the same substance . . .
but at least they are different in qualities, indeed as different in kind
as any two sets of qualities. (Ewing 1962, 110)

In thinking about Ewing's point, I imagine talking to this
distinguished philosopher, a fellow of the British Academy
and a lecturer at Cambridge, in my backyard in California.
"Grab a red-hot coal from your charcoal grill!" he challenges
me. "Hold it in your hand and observe carefully the searing
unendurable pain that arises in your consciousness. Does
that seem anything like a brain state?" I am so sure that he
has the empirical facts right that I grant his premises without
even performing the experiment. Leibniz and Ewing draw
forcefully to our attention the fact that *having* an experience
is quite unlike what one supposes *perceiving* a brain state or
process would be like; they conclude that experiences and
thoughts are not brain states or processes. Can we grant the
premise but avoid the conclusion?

If we imagine following Ewing's directions, it goes something like this. We are feeling an intense pain. We focus on
that pain and on a certain aspect of it. Not on its cause, nor
on the injury it might lead to, but on *what it is like to have it*.
This aspect of the experience is sometimes called its "subjective character," and such aspects are sometimes called "qualia." We focus on this aspect of the pain, and as we focus on it
we think, "This feeling is . . ." Then we imagine filling in the
right-hand side of this identity with any way we can imagine
apprehending a brain state. Perhaps we imagine seeing the
inside of a brain, as in *Fantastic Voyage:* or we imagine having
Herbert Feigl's imaginary instrument, the autocerebroscope,

which allows one to examine one's own brain while using it (Feigl 1967). We focus on a certain state presented to us in one of these ways and think of it as "that brain state." So we think, "This feeling is that brain state." And this strikes us, according to Ewing, as perfectly absurd. Or perhaps we imagine identifying the brain state in some less direct but more probable way, as for example as the state the onset of which corresponds to a sudden blip on the monitor of an instrument. Or perhaps we imagine a label or description of a brain state that we have read about in books or studied in classes: the brain state so-and-so. It will strike us as absurd, according to Ewing, that our thought or supposition, "This feeling is the brain state so-and-so," could be true.

The absurdity will derive from how much the properties we notice—the subjective characters of our experience—differ from the ones that we imagine seeing or reading about. To say that *this*, the feeling I am aware of when I, so to speak, look inward, is *that*, the thing I read about, just seems crazy. This feeling is what I will call the "Ewing intuition," and the argument based on it, the "experience gap argument": *this* could not be *a brain state*, because the gap between what it is like and what brain states are like is simply too large.

1.2   The Dialectic of Identity

A modern philosopher might pause before giving into the Ewing intuition and the experience gap argument, for at least three reasons. First, of course, is the wide acceptance of various forms of physicalism. If everything that goes on in the universe is physical, then my consciousness must be physical, and this feeling must be physical, however odd that may seem. And many smart people think that everything that goes on in the universe is physical. One really ought to hesitate, just on general principles, before rejecting this doctrine.

In addition to this somewhat ideological doubt, two related technical problems about the argument will immediately strike a philosopher. The first is that the candidate thought is an identity, and Frege has taught us all that identity gives rise to difficult problems (Frege 1960). Frege was particularly interested in what it is that informative identity statements convey. If the statement "This sensation is that brain state" is true, it is just such an informative identity statement—not only informative, but at least according to Ewing and Leibniz, absolutely astounding. Philosophers know that the minority of their number who have thought long and hard about the difference between "Tully is Tully" and "Tully is Cicero" have yet to reach agreement on the right thing to say, and that the pages and passions devoted to this problem by analytical philosophers in the twentieth century compare to those devoted to the many problems one might have thought to be both more important and more difficult, like, for example, the existence of God, the basis of personal identity, or the nature of virtue. Philosophers naturally hesitate before accepting any argument, however strong its intuitive pull, that turns on rejecting an identity statement. And of course in this particular case at least one part of the informative identity statement involves a demonstrative, "*this* feeling." Demonstratives and indexicals provide additional puzzles.

Second, not only identity statements, but also the relation of identity itself, presents problems. Identity is simply that relation an object has to itself and to no other; it is the relation that holds between a and b when there is just one thing that is both a and b. If a and b are identical, then they must share properties, for there is only one thing whose properties are at issue. It seems then that it is a small matter to prove nonidentity; one simply finds a property a has and b does not to show that a is not b. This is just the strategy a defense attorney might follow to show that the defendant was not the criminal. If the attorney can place the defendant in Toledo, say, at a time when the criminal had to be in Dubuque, she should win the case.

At first glance, this makes things look pretty good for the Ewing intuition. The properties that we find in the state of which we are subjectively aware, the feeling of pain, seem quite different than the ones associated with any brain states identified physically. The brain state will involve certain parts of the brain, for example, whereas my feeling of pain seems to be located in my hand insofar as it has a bodily location. The pain is quite intense and unpleasant. But what would make a brain state intense or unpleasant?

At second glance there is a problem, however. It is not enough to show that the properties we discover about a, thought about in one way, are quite different than those we associate with b, thought about in another way. We must show that a clearly lacks a property b has. Somewhat paradoxically, the more unlike a and b seem to be at first glance, the harder this may be to show. In particular, one has to keep in mind a fact that seems at first quite odd. Although the truth of the statement "$a = b$" requires something pretty important of a and b, it doesn't require much of anything about "a" and "b," other than that there is a single thing to which they both refer. "a" does not need to be definable in terms of "b," or to have been introduced in terms of "b," or to involve properties that supervene on those that "b" involves, or vice versa. In this sense, identity is a very *weak* relation.

Consider, for example, claims that one individual, existing at one time, is the reincarnation of what appears to be another individual, living at another time. The present Dalai Lama, for example, is claimed to be the reincarnation of the previous Dalai Lama, who died some years before the current one was born. Reincarnation is supposed to be a matter of being the same person, the same consciousness, surviving in a different body. Suppose one says, "Well, the fourteenth Dalai Lama is clearly not the thirteenth Dalai Lama, since the thirteenth had many properties the fourteenth does not have. The thirteenth is dead, was born in the nineteenth century, and lived in Tibet his whole life; the fourteenth is alive, was born in the twentieth century, and has lived in China and India as well as in Tibet." To this it can be easily replied, "The fourteenth was also born in the nineteenth century, born then in his previous incarnation. The thirteenth has also lived in India; he has been living there in his present incarnation." Once one accepts the possibility of reincarnation, then one naturally makes some logical distinctions and adds parameters to various empirical predicates. A person lives a certain time *in a certain body*; a person is born at a given time *in a given incarnation*; a person dies *in one incarnation* but is born *in another*, and so forth. Instead of a number of properties that the thirteenth Dalai Lama has and the fourteenth does not, we find more complicated conditions that both Dalai Lamas share, the apparent differences residing in the parameters associated with two different ways of thinking of the same object. "The fourteenth Dalai Lama" is a way of thinking of the Dalai Lama via his present reincarnation, "the thirteenth Dalai Lama" a way of thinking of him via his previous incarnation. We may doubt that looking at things in this way is right, but it is hard to argue that it is inconsistent. The fourteenth Dalai Lama, energetic, robust, and living in

India, strikes us as being quite different, in innumerable ways, from the thirteenth Dalai Lama, a lifelong resident of Tibet, long dead. But a simple appeal to the logic of identity and the properties the Dalai Lamas were observed to have will not suffice to dispose of a doctrine defended by subtle distinctions and explanations accumulated over the centuries of Tibetan Buddhism. One needs to argue the case on more substantive grounds involving the nature of personal identity, what would be required for reincarnation, and the physical basis of memory.

Ewing's statement that the conscious and the physical are as different as sight and sound suggests another more relevant example. Molyneaux posed a famous problem to John Locke: if a blind man were suddenly able to see, could he tell, merely by looking, before any experience of correlation, that when he looked at a sphere, he was seeing the same shape with which he was familiar by touch? Locke agreed with Molyneaux's conjecture that he could not. That is, the truth of the thought, "This (seen) shape is this (felt) shape," would be a surprising but true identity. What could be more unlike than vision and touch (Locke 1694: bk. I, chap. IX)?

But the analogy is imperfect in an important way. In the Molyneaux case we have one property or state of a physical object: sphericity. And we have two sensations, quite unlike. The sensations are not one and the same; it is what they are sensations *of* that is one and the same. Suppose Arthur and Raquel are in my brain having visual sensations of the various things going on there. I have the sensation of pain. The question is not whether their visual sensations and my pain sensation are sensations *of* the same thing. It is rather whether my sensation itself, the pain, is that state, property, or process that their visual sensations are *of*. Is the pain I have the brain state they observe?

The Molyneaux problem in fact seems to suggest a dualist view, similar to Ewing's, a double-aspect theory. One thing, a state or process in my brain, has two quite different aspects: its physical aspect, which explains what Arthur and Raquel see and what makes it fit the descriptions of neurophysiologists, and its mental aspect, the sensations that arise in the mind of the person whose brain state it is. As Ewing said, "The physiological and the mental characteristics may conceivably belong to the same substance . . . but at least they are different in qualities, indeed as different in kind as any two sets of qualities" (Ewing 1962, 110). In contemporary debates about dualism, this sort of *property* dualism is usually at issue, and that will be our topic in this book. Can the property of being in a certain brain state be the very same property as that of having a certain sensation? Can this (type of) feeling be identical with this (type of) brain state?

A simple appeal to the logic of identity and the Ewing intuition will not suffice to prove even property dualism. Nor will a simple appeal to the possibility of informative and even surprising but true identities refute it. The question still remains: can we really make sense of the thought that *this feeling*, this aspect of what goes on inside me that makes it a toothache or a headache or the smell of a gardenia or the taste of turnips, is an aspect of my brain that someone else, a miniature Raquel or Arthur, could, in principle, see?

I will argue that we can. The bulk of my argument will be directed against three arguments from contemporary analytical philosophers that I see as sophisticated developments of and variations on the experience gap argument: the zombie argument, the knowledge argument, and the modal argument. I call the position that these arguments support *neo-dualism*.

1.3 The Zombie Argument

The zombie argument, on which I focus in chapter 4, maintains that there is a possible world inhabited by beings that are physically indiscernible from us but are not conscious. It is a key argument of an important recent book by David Chalmers, *The Conscious Mind* (Chalmers 1996). What zombies lack and we have are the subjective characters of our experience, to which Ewing calls our attention. Chalmers uses the term "qualia" and conceives of qualia as a nonphysical, causally impotent layer of brainstate attributes. These attributes of our brain states are not *identical* with any physical attributes of our brain states. And there are no combinations of physical attributes of brain states from which it follows as a matter of logic that they have these nonphysical ones (i.e., qualia *do not logically supervene on physical states of the brain*). Chalmers acknowledges that as a matter of fact, the way the world works, if two brains are physically indiscernible, their states will have the same qualia. But this is a fact of nature, not of metaphysics or logic (i.e., qualia *do naturally supervene on the physical states of the brain*). These qualia are the "what-it-is-like properties." For us, it is like something to be in pain. It hurts. For zombies in zombie-pain, it is not like anything. There is a state that zombies go into when they cut themselves or stub their toes. This state makes them do the things we do when we are in pain. They curse and jump up and down and hold the injured part. This state functions exactly like our state of pain, but they do not feel what we do; they do not have the conscious experience. Since the zombies are physically exactly like us but have no conscious experiences, having a conscious experience must not be a physical property.

The focus on the what-it-is-like properties in recent debates about physicalism dates from an article by Thomas Nagel, which was largely responsible for rescuing these "subjective characters" from marginalization at the hands of physicalists: "—the fact that an organism has conscious experiences AT ALL means, basically, that there is something it is like to be that organism. . . . We may call this the subjective character of experience" (Nagel 1974, 519; see also Farrell 1950; Feigl 1967, 139–140). Nagel was reacting to various versions of physicalism that seem to ignore subjective characters. This tradition has its roots in a sort of sophisticated logical behaviorism of the 1950s, different versions of which were inspired by the works of Ryle and Wittgenstein. On these views, mental states were something like dispositions to behave. In the 1960s and 1970s, influenced by the ideas of Feigl, Place, and Smart, David Lewis and David Armstrong independently developed an elegant version of the identity theory, which Armstrong dubbed "central-state materialism." This was a really new proposal in the history of the mind-body problem. The main idea was to accept that mental states were internal states conceived in terms of the ways those who are in them are disposed to behave. Dispositions to behave are grounded by (or perhaps simply are) internal states. So mental states are not behavioral states; rather, they are internal states *known by* the behavior they are apt to cause, or, more generally, by their typical causal role. They are the occupants of causal roles postulated by "folk psychology." These occupants are, as a matter of fact, brain states.

This theory developed a version of an important idea of Smart's: that our concept of mental states is "topic-neutral." That is, folk psychology, everything we need to know to use our mental concepts to describe and explain our own mental life and that of others, is compatible with the view that mental states are physical or that they are nonphysical but entails neither. We know mental states as the typical effects of certain things and the typical causes of others. Pain is a typical effect of unusual pressures on the surface of the body and a typical cause of crying, complaining, limping, and so forth. It has turned out to be overwhelmingly plausible that this state is, in fact, a physical state of the brain and not, say, a state of some nonextended Cartesian mind or a nonphysical state of brains. The Lewis-Armstong view explained how we could have topic-neutral concepts of straightforwardly physical states: the concepts were descriptive concepts of the occupants of causal roles. The essential property that makes the state a mental state is a neutral, relational property.

Many philosophers felt that such a causal/functional analysis of our concepts of mental states was basically correct but that something less dramatic than identity would be more plausible as the relation between mental states and brain states. If we suppose that beings with a quite different physical constitution than we—Martians evolved in basically different ways than we, terrestrial animals on a quite different evolutionary branch, robots built of silicon, metal, and plastic, for example—can have mental states, then we will not want to identify those states with the particular physical basis they find in us. The most widely accepted view, by the late 1970s and 1980s, was a weakened form of the identity theory: mental states are in some sense functional states that *supervene* on brain states; that is, any two brains in the same physical states were in the same mental states, but not necessarily vice versa.

Nagel's emphasis on subjective characters was a note of disagreement, or at least worried hesitation, in the midst of an emerging physicalist consensus. It simply didn't seem credible that subjective characters, or qualia, could be given a functional analysis. And so, it seemed, there was no clear way to conceive of them as being brain states. Nagel's aim seemed less to provide an alternative account of mind than to observe that deep and important puzzles had not yet been solved.

Chalmers, following Block, provides a useful way of looking at this and introduces some terminology I will adopt:

[There are] two quite distinct concepts of mind. The first is the *phenomenal* concept of mind. This is the concept of mind as conscious experience, and of a mental state as a consciously experienced mental state. . . . The second is the *psychological* concept of mind. This is the concept of mind as the causal or explanatory basis for behavior. A state is mental in this sense if it plays the right sort of role in the explanation of behavior. According to the psychological concept, it matters little whether a mental state has a conscious quality or not. What matters is the role it plays in a cognitive economy.

On the phenomenal concept, mind is characterized by the way it *feels*; on the psychological concept, mind is characterized by what it *does*. There should be no question of competition between these two notions of mind. Neither of them is *the* correct analysis of mind. They cover different phenomena, both of which are quite real. (Chalmers 1996, 11; see also Block 1995a; Feigl 1967)

On Chalmers' view, then, the Wittgenstein-Ryle-Smart-Lewis-Armstrong-Fodor functionalist tradition has something right: it has provided increasingly sophisticated treatments of the *psychological* concept of mind. The error is in supposing that the same treatment could be extended to the phenomenal concept or supposing that, if it could not be extended, the phenomenal concept was simply confused. If we accept Chalmers' distinction, then it seems there could be beings who were psychologically like us but phenomenally different. They might have different experiences than we do, or they might have no experiences at all (e.g., zombies). But the Chalmers zombie argument is supposed to show something further than this possibility. My zombie twin is not simply psychologically like me, in Chalmers' sense. It is also *physically indiscernible* from me. The possibility of such a being would show not only that my zombie twin and I can be psychologically alike while phenomenally different but also that we can be *physically alike* while phenomenally different. I'll argue in chapter 4 that we have no reason to take this extra step and that the zombie argument fails as an argument against physicalism.

As a backup, Chalmers uses a version of the inverted spectrum argument. This is a new use of an old philosophical thought experiment that involves asking oneself how one knows that when another person sees a red object, she has the same kind of sensation—the same thing going on in her mind—as one has in one's own mind when seeing a red object. Couldn't it be that you see what I would call green when you see red objects and associate the word "red" with that sensation?

The thought experiment was originally supposed to show that logical behaviorism was wrong, because there could be a mental difference without a behavioral difference. This use of the argument is neutral on the issue of physicalism and dualism, for a physicalist need not be a logical behaviorist.

Recently Ned Block and others have used basically the same hypothesis as a refutation of functionalism about qualia.[1] The argument is that inverted qualia are possible, with no difference in behavior and also no difference in functional organization. Functional properties cannot distinguish the different subjective characters; hence functionalism is wrong about phenomenal mental states. This is consistent with maintaining, as Block does, that it may be a good theory for intentional states.

Neither of these thought experiments requires that the two subjects whose qualia are inverted relative to one another be in exactly the same physical states, either in the same or in different possible worlds. Chalmers' new use requires that we add this to the thought experiment. We have twins in different possible worlds, physically indiscernible, but with spectra that are inverted relative to one another. He claims that this is clearly possible and that this possibility shows that there could be a mental difference with no physical difference whatsoever. If there can be such a mental difference without a physical difference, then subjective characters are nonphysical aspects of humans. I will argue, however, that the inverted spectrum argument fails for the same reasons that the zombie argument does.

1.4   The Knowledge Argument

In his original article, Nagel more or less formulates an argument that has come to be known as "the knowledge argument." Frank Jackson develops it in a series of articles. In "What Mary Didn't Know" (Jackson 1997), on which I will focus, he considers a person, Mary, who is trapped in a black and white room. There she learns "everything there is to know about the physical nature of the world . . . she knows all the physical facts. . . . It seems, however, that Mary does not know all there is to know. For when she is let out of the black and white room . . . she will learn what it is like to see something red" (Jackson 1997, 567). Since Mary knows all the physical facts and then learns something new, there are more facts than physical facts, and so physicalism is false. That's the knowledge argument.

I accept the premises of the argument but do not think the conclusion follows. Mary does learn something when she steps from the black and white room and sees a ripe tomato or a fire hydrant. She does learn what it is like to see red, and this is not something she could pick up from the books she has read, even though they included all the physical facts about color and color vision and the related brain states.

The argument turns on the assumption that when we learn something about the world, we do so by coming to believe or know a fact we did not believe or know before. In chapter 5 I will argue that underlying this premise is a confused and oversimple conception of knowledge. And underlying this confusion, I will claim, is a distorted picture of the relation between knowledge and reality, between epistemology and metaphysics. When these issues are worked out, we can see that Mary's new knowledge is no threat to physicalism.

In chapter 6, I'll develop a contrasting picture of knowledge that will allow us to sort out some issues about objectivity and subjectivity. The perspective we gain will deepen our understanding not only of the knowledge argument but also of the zombie argument and ultimately of the experience gap argument of Leibniz and Ewing. Then, in chapter 7, I'll say what Mary learns.

1.5   The Modal Argument

The knowledge argument is an epistemic version of the experience gap argument: the idea of knowledge as a propositional attitude is used to bring out the intuition. We can think of the zombie and inverted spectrum arguments as modal versions of the experience gap argument. The Leibniz-Ewing intuition is bolstered by possible worlds and the concept of supervenience.

But if the contemplated relation between sensations and brain states is identity, as I will advocate, rather than supervenience, there is a simpler modal version of the argument, due to Kripke, that doesn't involve a world full of zombies or a wholesale shift of qualia (Kripke 1997). It simply involves focusing on one sensation and the brain state that the physicalist claims is identical with it. Kripke argues that if, as the identity theorist claims, the sensation is identical with the brain state or process, then it must be necessarily identical, since if A and B are in fact one thing, there is no possible world in which they are two things. Kripke claims, however, that even the physicalist admits that the relation between the brain state and the sensation is contingent or at the very least *seems* to be contingent. We can call this "Kripke's contingency." The usual explanation for the sense that an identity is contingent is that we are thinking of the contingent fact that the object in question fits the particular identifying criteria associated with one or the other of the terms. Whereas it is necessary that Hesperus is Phosphorus, it is contingent that Hesperus is seen in the morning, a condition we associate with the name "Phosphorus." Whereas it is necessary that water is H_2O, it is contingent that H_2O is the wet, drinkable stuff that flows in our rivers and falls from the sky, the criteria we associate with "water."

But there is no room for such an explanation of apparent contingency in the case of sensations and brain states. As we might say, in the midst of the Ewing experiment, pain is not something that *happens* to feel like *this*, but does so only contingently and in a different possible world might feel quite different. The relation between being pain and feeling like *this* is not at all like the relation between being H_2O and filling our ponds and lakes. H_2O might not fill that role, and something else might. But having *this* feeling is what it is to be in pain.

Since we cannot explain away Kripke's contingency by appealing to a contingent connection between the sensation and its usual identifying criteria, the simplest explanation for the feeling of contingency is contingency. But there is no contingent identity. So sensations are not brain states or processes.

In chapter 8 I will use the apparatus built up in the previous chapters to cope with Kripke's argument and a closely related argument used by Chalmers.

1.6   The Plan

My overall strategy will be to try to defend a version of physicalism that adopts our commonsense views about the reality and importance of the subjective character of experience. I call this "antecedent physicalism." I will then argue that the neo-dualist arguments foist upon physicalism doctrines that it need not and should not include. The zombie argument, I will claim, depends on denying the causal efficacy of experience, the commonsense view that our experiences have all sorts of important physical effects. This denial, the doctrine of epiphenomenalism, has no warrant in common sense, and the antecedent physicalist has no reason whatsoever to adopt it. The zombie argument also depends on supposing that subjective characters cannot be identified with physical states but at most *supervene* on them. The antecedent physicalist has no reason to adopt this view either.

With the knowledge argument and the modal arguments, it is helpful to put the debate in the context of Frege's problem about informative identities. It seems common sense that the reason a true thought of the form "*A* is *B*" might be informative, although "*A* is *A*" is not, is that the former involves two different ways of thinking of the same object; the information is simply that these *are* two ways of thinking of the same object. There can be two ways of thinking of properties and states, not only of things. I can think of the color of blood as "the color of blood" or as "red" or, while attending to a red object, as "this color."

When Mary leaves the Jackson room and sees a red tomato, she is in a position for the first time to think of the color red as "this color" and in a position for the first time to think of the sensation people have when they see red as "this sensation." Surely, then, her new knowledge ought to be accounted for by this new way of thinking, not by a new object thought about. And similarly, the contingency that one has in mind when one supposes that, say, pain might not be stimulated C-fibers must be explained by the two ways of thinking involved. If the physicalist can explain the knowledge in the one case, and the possibility in the other, by appeal to two ways of thinking of a single state, he ought to be able to block the inference that there must two states, a brain state and a nonphysical state, to account for Mary's knowledge, or Kripke's contingency. I'll call this the "two-ways" strategy.

There is an imposing obstacle to this simple and seemingly straightforward strategy. Mary is *not* thinking about her ways of thinking about color sensations but about the sensations themselves; they are what her new knowledge is about. To find the content of her new knowledge, we seem to require two things, not merely two ways of thinking about one thing, and the physicalist does not have two things to offer. Kripke doesn't (simply) think that there is a contingent connection between his way of thinking about brain states and his ways of thinking about pain; they are parts of his thought, but not what that thought is about. To get at the contingency, we seem to require two states, not simply two ways of thinking about one state. And this the physicalist cannot provide.

This objection to the two-ways strategy is imposing, but I will claim it is mistaken. At the root of this objection, and at the roots of the knowledge argument and the modal argument, and ultimately at the root of the zombie argument too, is a mistake about the structure of knowledge and possibility, a mistake I call the "subject matter fallacy." This is the fallacy of supposing that *the* content of a statement or a belief consists in the conditions that the truth of the statement or belief puts on the objects and properties the statement or belief is about. Consider my belief that Hillary Clinton is a resident of New York. The subject matter of this belief is the things and conditions (properties, relations) it is about: Hillary Clinton, the state of New York, and the relation of being a resident of. For the belief to be true, these objects have to meet certain conditions: the first two must bear the third to one another; that is, Hillary Clinton must be a resident of New York. It is quite natural, then, to take the proposition that Hillary Clinton is a resident of New York to be *the* content of the belief. And if my thought were not a belief but merely the entertaining of a possibility, then it would be natural to take the proposition that Hillary Clinton is a resident of New York as the possibility I entertain.

But for certain kinds of thoughts, this is a mistake. Suppose, for example, that Hillary Clinton has the thought that she would express with "I am a resident of New York." The subject matter content of this thought is the very same proposition, that Hillary Clinton is a resident of New York, for when Hillary Clinton thinks "I" she thinks about herself, and when she says "I" she refers to herself. But that content of the statement or thought does not get at a very special aspect of it: the fact that it is the sort of thought one has about oneself. To get at that aspect, we need to bring in, in addition to the subject matter content, what I call the "reflexive contents" of the thoughts or statements. These contents are *not* merely conditions on the subject matter but conditions on the utterances or thoughts *themselves*. Hillary's statement *S*, "I am a resident of New York," can be true only if *S itself* is spoken by a resident of New York. Hillary's thought *T*, which she expresses with this statement, can be true only if the thinker of *T itself* is a resident of New York.

Not only for thoughts about oneself or statements that use indexicals do we need to appeal to reflexive contents, however. We also need to appeal to reflexive contents whenever we want to understand how thoughts connect with perception and action. All three arguments depend on real and robust intuitions about what might be the case or what someone might know. A philosophy that is wedded to the subject matter assumption can find these possibilities only in a world with some extra subject matter, and that extra subject matter is what dualism provides. The subject matter assumption has vague connections with some varieties of objectivity. I shall argue, however, that it is not entailed by any kind of objectivity to which physicalists ought to be committed.

I will argue, then, that two of our three arguments derive what power they have from trying to make a subject matter content do the work of a reflexive content. I'll try simply to give the flavor of my argument here. Consider the knowledge argument. Mary has a thought that she would express with "This is what it is like to see red." This statement expresses new knowledge. Can a physicalist, someone who believes, let's say, that the subjective feel of Mary's brain state is a certain neurological property—let's call it "B_{52}"—account for this new knowledge?

The new knowledge should correspond to the content of the statement that expresses it. The subject matter content of this statement, according to the physicalist, will simply be that B_{52} (the referent of "this sensation") is the subjective character of the state people are in when they see red. But this knowledge can't be what Mary learned. This knowledge does not require the experience of seeing red; in fact, it is something she should have already known from her studies in the Jackson room. The physicalist has a dilemma: either deny that Mary has new knowledge or accept that the new knowledge involves a new bit of subject matter, a nonphysical aspect of her brain state, about which she knew nothing in her black and white room.

The problem, as I diagnose it, is that Mary's new knowledge cannot be identified with the subject matter content of the statement with which she expresses it, nor with the subject matter content of the thought with which she thinks it. Mary's new epistemic state, the one she expresses with "This is what it is like to see red," is of a certain type. States of this type are true only if the aspect of brain states to which their possessors attend is the aspect of brain states that normal people have in normal conditions when they see red. That is the reflexive content of her thought, and that is her new knowledge.

I will argue that we cannot account for certain kinds of knowledge and certain kinds of conception if we confine ourselves to subject matter contents. The neo-dualists' arguments each use this fact as a motivation for countenancing a nonphysical property, which will allow us to identify the thing known or conceived. The key is not to confine ourselves to subject matter contents.

That, then, is a glimpse of my strategy. The strategy will, I hope, appear more promising to the reader as the argument unfolds than it may at this point. The plan, then, is this. In the next two chapters, I will explain antecedent physicalism.

First I'll say what I mean by physicalism. Then I'll develop what I take to be a (fairly) commonsense view about subjective characters and consciousness. I will end by listing some metaphysical and epistemological doctrines to avoid: epiphenomenalism, misplaced functionalism, and the doctrine of subject matter. These are not part of antecedent physicalism and are in fact not very plausible. Then I will argue in chapters that follow that the zombie argument, the knowledge argument, and the modal argument pose no threat to antecedent physicalism; the illusion that they do is based on the mistaken view that physicalism entails the discarded doctrines. This mistaken view is itself hidden by inadequate but widely accepted conceptions of the structure of knowledge and possibility.

2   Sentience and Thought

Feigl: *Wouldn't the qualities of immediate experience be left out in a perfect physical representation of the universe?*

Einstein: *Why without them, the world would be nothing but a pile of [dirt]!*

—As reported in Herbert Feigl, The "Mental" and the "Physical": The Essay and a Postscript

I don't want to suggest that there is nothing very persuasive about the arguments we will consider. But although there is something persuasive about them, I don't think we need to be persuaded. I'd like to draw an analogy here to a situation in the philosophy of religion. I think that Hume said just the right thing about the problem of evil in the Eleventh Dialogue of his *Dialogues Concerning Natural Religion* (Hume 1779). If someone comes upon all of the evil in the world mixed with all the good in the world, the thought of a perfect God, all-powerful and perfectly benevolent, would never suggest itself. The reasonable hypothesis would be an intelligent but imperfect and indifferent creator or perhaps a committee of imperfect and indifferent creators. But if you came to these facts *antecedently convinced* of the classic God

of Western monotheism, infinitely or at least overwhelmingly perfect and definitely benevolent, the existence of evil
would not logically refute your view. The reason is that you
would not assume you understand the plan that such a Being had in mind—to do so would be to commit the sin of
pride—and unless you assumed you understood the plan,
you couldn't be sure that the evil you observed wasn't a
necessary part of a plan an all-powerful or at least extraordi-
narily powerful God might come up with (see Perry 1999).

I regard myself as someone with an antecedent belief
in physicalism facing the problem of subjective characters
with considerable humility about my knowledge of what
the physical world might be capable of and what science
might someday be able to explain.

2.1   Antecedent Physicalism

With the exception of headaches, there is nothing at all about
what it is like to have experiences, in and of itself, that would
suggest to one that they are states of the brain. Focusing on
our experiences and mental states and asking the question
of what sort of things they might be is something we may
do for the first time in an introductory philosophy class—
perhaps reading Descartes' *Meditations*. It does not seem that
we are encountering our own brains' states. But that does
not mean that if one is antecedently convinced that mental
states are states of the brain, dwelling on what it is like to
have experiences should persuade one to give up that view
or to deny, as some physicalists think they must, that experiences and their subjective characters have a straightforward
and robust existence.

Perhaps it would be better to say "prima facie physicalist"
rather than "antecedent physicalist." I do not have in mind

a complete dogmatist for whom physicalism is a religious principle, as my reference to Hume's analysis in his *Dialogues* might suggest. I simply mean someone who is committed to physicalism in the sense that she or he sees some compelling reasons for it and will not give it up without seeing some clear reason to do so. The question for such person is not whether physicalism is the most natural account of the subjective character of experience but whether it offers a possible account. The advocates of the zombie argument, the knowledge argument, and the modal argument say that it does not. The arguments purport to show that there are important aspects of experiences, their subjective characters, that *cannot* be accommodated by physicalism. If physicalism cannot accommodate the subjective character of experience, one must either give up physicalism or deny the subjective character of experience—and some physicalists have felt compelled to deny the existence of qualia or diminish them in some way (see Dennett 1988; Lewis 1990).

The position of the antecedent physicalist is different. We grant that there are subjective characters—so long as qualia or subjective characters are not *defined* as nonphysical. Indeed, we insist on the importance of the subjective character of experience. We then construct the best account, or at least a reasonably natural account, of subjective characters on the assumption that they are physical. Then, and only then, do we look at the neo-dualist arguments to see if they point out some inadequacy or hidden contradiction in our account.

In the dialectic of philosophy there are many quite different situations in which one can find oneself. Sometimes one is trying to persuade someone with quite different views and presuppositions that a certain thing is so. In such a case, one must set aside much of what one believes, all the controversial assumptions, and search for a common beginning point.

The situation is quite different when one defends one's own view from a charge of inconsistency, incoherence, or inadequacy. In this case, it makes no sense to jettison your own view, the view whose consistency or adequacy you are defending. You want to rely on the distinctions and concepts that your view provides to counter the criticism, and you have every right to do so.

I view myself as being in the second dialectical situation. Neo-dualists claim that physicalists cannot account for the subjective character of experience and that to attempt to do so leads to incoherence or inconsistency. The best way to reply to these arguments is to work out a physicalist approach to the phenomena in question and then see if the arguments of the neo-dualists show any inadequacies, incoherencies, or inconsistencies in that approach.

So what I will do is put forward a set of views that a physicalist might hold, views that do not, so far as I can see, in any way deny the data of experience. Then I will look at the three arguments and see if there is anything in them that should cause such an antecedently convinced physicalist to abandon her or his doctrine.

Antecedent physicalism is the result of a two-step procedure. First one lists the salient facts about mental states, both psychological and phenomenal, that seem to be the basis for the way we experience these states, recognize them in others, and use them to organize a large part of our lives. This is what I'll call, somewhat hopefully, "common sense." Then one adds the fact (or hypothesis) that these states are physical and accepts the consequences that follow from that assumption.

One thus formulates antecedent physicalism without even a sidelong glance at the arguments of dualists—well, perhaps a glance or two is necessary to know what issues to worry about. Then one asks, "Is there any reason I should give up this combination of common sense and physicalism? Is there anything I have left out? Is there any hidden (or not so hidden) contradiction or incoherence in my view?" My basic claim in this book is that the three arguments we consider do not provide such a reason.

2.2   Physicalism and Materialism

By "physical" I mean, following Feigl, the types and concepts and laws that suffice in principle for the explanation and prediction of inorganic processes. In his more careful formulations, which take account of the possibility of some sort of emergence, Feigl distinguished between "$physical_1$" and "$physical_2$":

> By "$physical_1$ terms" I mean *all* (empirical) terms whose specification of meaning essentially involves logical (necessary or, more usually, probabilistic) connections with the intersubjective observation language, as well as the terms of this observation language itself. Theoretical concepts in physics, biology, psychology, and the social sciences hence are all—at least—$physical_1$ concepts. By "$physical_2$" I mean the kind of theoretical concepts (and statements) regarding the inorganic (lifeless) domain of nature. (Feigl 1967, 57)

Feigl thought it likely that the two concepts coincided, and progress in physical chemistry and the discovery and analyses of DNA have supported his opinion. I don't have anything positive of substance to add about physicalism, and the reader can substitute more up-to-date definitions with no loss. I will, at the end of the next chapter, have some things to say about what physicalism does not entail.

Many physicalists refer to themselves as "materialists." Materialism is a more common word and has pleasant historical connections with radical thinkers of the seventeenth and eighteenth century, some of whom were persecuted for their atheism and general antiestablishment views. Physicalism is hardly an antiestablishment view these days. More importantly, there is a big difference between what the physical world was thought to be like three centuries ago and what we are now told about it. Materialism is really the physicalism of the eighteenth century, when it was assumed that the fundamental physical properties were basically shape, size, and motion, the primary qualities of Galileo, Newton, Boyle, and Locke. These are familiar qualities and afford intuitive arguments of various sorts about divisibility and the like. None of these intuitions or the arguments founded on them can be transferred without argument to the fundamental physical properties of today's physics, which are for the most part neither familiar nor intuitive. With that preface, let us turn to the first step of antecedent physicalism.

2.3 Common Sense about the Mind

I'll organize what I take to be common sense about the mind into two categories: what common sense takes conscious states to be and how common sense thinks we know about them—that is, the commonsense metaphysics and epistemology of mental states.

A good place to start is the British empiricists; they claimed to be paying attention to what was going on in the mind, were quite unembarrassed by it, and didn't have to pretend their studies were a species of mental linguistics. Locke, Berkeley, and Hume all at least implicitly make a distinction, among the things that go on in our mind, between those involved in sensation and those involved in thought. Hume's distinction between impressions and ideas is explicit and central to his philosophy. Impressions are sensations and passions, that is, physical pains and pleasures, sensations involved in perception, bodily sensations, anger and joy and other emotions that have a clear feel to them. Ideas are thoughts and components of thoughts. When I hit my thumb with a hammer, the pain I feel is an impression. When I remember doing so, anticipate doing so (for it happens at least once in any project that requires hammering nails), write about doing so, and the like, I don't have the impression, I employ the idea. Impressions are the "raw feels" of Feigl; they are something it is like to have; they have "subjective characters." A world without them would be, as Einstein said, just a pile of [dirt].

Hume thinks that ideas are like impressions but less vivid. When I hit my thumb with a hammer, the pain I feel is an impression. When I remember this later or worry about doing it again, it is the idea that is involved in my thought. There is both a semantic and a phenomenological relation between the idea and the impression. The idea is *of* the impression; the thought is *about* the impression. The memories and fears we have that involve the idea of pain are memories and fears of having the impression, but the impression is not itself a part of the thought. These are semantical facts, facts about what the idea stands for and the contents of the thoughts of which it is a part. But also, as Hume says, the idea *resembles* the impression. We may not like the term "resembles," but there seems to be no denying that there is an uncanny, phenomenologically primitive and firm link between our idea of pain and our experience of pain. The situation is quite unlike that of the word "pain." We can easily imagine that word sounding just as it does, spelled just as it is, standing for something else, even something quite pleasurable. It is not easy to imagine our thoughts that involve our idea of pain being just as they are, but being about the taste of chocolate chip cookies, say, rather than the feeling of pain.

I will distinguish between our Humean idea of pain and our concept of pain. Concepts are rather heterogeneous mental structures that are systematically involved in picking up and storing information from perception and discourse, processing information, imagining, remembering, planning, daydreaming, and every other activity that counts as, or involves, thinking. Image-like ideas of the sort Hume focuses on are important parts of concepts, but there is a lot more to them. Hume was after what Chalmers calls the "phenomenological concept of pain" and I will call the "phenomenological part of the concept of pain." What Chalmers calls the psychological concept of pain is another part of our ordinary concept. We think that pain has typical causes and effects. When we see the nurse's needle approaching our arm, we see his movement as a typical cause of pain in the possessor of the arm in question, and if it is ours, we anticipate feeling pain and perhaps resolve to stifle some of its typical effects, so as not to cry out, run, or say rude things to the nurse.

A person can have a concept of a sensation she has never had. A person blind from birth can realize that others have visual sensations and understand very well how they function. A person may believe that the sensation of tasting chocolate chip cookies is quite wonderful and travel a great distance to experience it for the first time. And a person can have a concept of a sensation without knowing its name, its causes, or its function, if any. In the example above of getting a shot from a nurse, the various components of my concept of pain worked seamlessly together: I knew its name, I knew what it was like, I knew its causes, I knew its effects. The examples of this paragraph show that this unity is not always present. There is room for significant gains in knowledge about sensations of which we have a concept. I can learn the name of this funny taste in my mouth; I can learn what it's like to taste chocolate chip cookies; I can learn the typical causes of depression.

The various parts of our concepts of sensations are not all equal. For a number of sensations, including the sensation of pain, there is what I will call a demonstrative/recognitional core to the ordinary concept. A person who has such a concept will be able to recognize the sensation of pain when he is having it; he will be able to attend to it and think of it as "this sensation," and he will be more confident of the judgment that he expresses, in such a situation, with the words "This sensation is pain" than he will be of anything else about pain. This structure of our concept of pain is, I think, clearly behind Ewing's strategy. He thinks we will be most clear about the nature of pain if we are actually having it, or at least reminding ourselves forcefully and vividly about what it is like to have it, and in that situation, he assumes, we will be least likely to suppose something as silly as that pain might be a state of a brain.

So more or less following Hume, there are two basic kinds of goings-on in the mind, which I'll call "experiences" and "thoughts." The capacities for these I'll call "sentience" and "thought." It's like something to have sensations. It is sometimes like something to have thoughts. We have sensory images, including inner voices, that are intimately involved in some kinds of thinking, especially remembering, imagining, mentally rehearsing, planning, and anticipating. Merely having concepts and beliefs is not like much of anything, but using the ideas and formulating the beliefs is often like something. My picture then is a modification of Hume's. It's like something to have sensations of all sorts, and it is also like something to have images or Humean ideas of various sorts before one's mind. But lots of ideation and thought isn't like anything, and our concepts are heterogeneous structures that may or may not contain such ideas and images.

Most experiences involve some thought, and most thoughts involve some experience. When I hit my thumb with the hammer, the pain was pretty pure, but the anger was sensation mixed with thought of being an idiot. The thought itself had an experiential side, as my inner voice said to me, "You idiot!"

All that is important is that my neo-Humean framework is intuitive enough for the reader to follow. If my arguments against neo-dualists are correct, the main points should survive translation into any more plausible and sophisticated frameworks that can be drawn from modern cognitive science.

I take the distinction between sentience and thought to be closely related to Ned Block's distinction between phenomenal consciousness and other kinds of consciousness, especially access-consciousness. I follow Block in spirit if not always in detail on a number of other issues also, including skepticism about functionalist analyses of sentience and sympathy with functionalist analyses of thought, and consider myself a Blockean with respect to many issues of mental metaphysics (Block 1995a; see also Feigl 1967).

Epistemologically, my position is similar to that of Brian Loar, as developed in his article "Phenomenal States" (Loar 1990), and that of William Lycan, as developed in his article "A Limited Defense of Phenomenal Information" (Lycan 1995). Both Loar and Lycan develop versions of the two-ways strategy. (Loar and Block at least appear to disagree on the matter of the possibility of functional analyses of sentience; I side with Block.) The chief innovations of the present work have to do with the development of the concept of *reflexive content* and its application to the issues involved.[2]

Before saying more about the metaphysics of the mind, I need to say a bit about how I use the word "state." First, "state" can be used for a particular event, or for a universal, a type of state in the first sense. In the particular sense, the brain state I am in now will never happen again. In the universal or type sense, you might be in the same state now, or I might be in the same state later. The types in question can deal with very abstract issues or very concrete ones. Two engines might be in the same rather abstract state in that they are both running, but in quite different, more concrete states in that the pressures in their intake manifolds are different. The term is sometimes used to mean a total state, so that if you know what state an object is in at a given time, you know all the relevant properties it has at that time, as when we talk about *the* state of a system at that time. I use the term to mean a partial state, so that the state of an object at a time determines only some of its properties at that time. If by "state" we mean a relatively concrete total type, it is logically possible but quite unlikely that I would ever be in the same state twice. If we mean a relatively abstract partial type, then it presumably happens all the time. In this sense, I am in a number of physical states right now, including weighing more than 180 pounds, having blood circulating in my brain, and so forth. You share many of these properties, although no doubt there are very many states we are not both in.

There is a certain flexibility in our talk about states, aspects of states, and exactly what a given state is a state of. Suppose Rose has puce-colored fingernails on her right hand. Being puce-colored is a state her nails are in. Having puce-colored fingernails is a state that Rose's fingers are in. Having a hand with such fingers is a state Rose is in. And that state is an aspect of many other, more comprehensive states Rose is in, including her total state.

Consider the pain I felt when I followed Ewing's directions and picked up a red-hot piece of charcoal from the grill. My having the pain, or being in pain, was a particular event, one that was caused by my picking up the charcoal and led to my dropping it quickly. The event involved my being in a certain state. Suppose that ϕ is the state brains are in when the possessors of those brains are in pain. Then we can say that ϕ was an aspect of the state of my brain, or that my brain was in state ϕ, or that I was in state ϕ', where ϕ' is the state of having a brain that is in state ϕ.

The term "aspect" of a brain state gives us even more flexibility than "state." Two complex brain states might have various physical substates in common—they might both involve some process in some part of the brain. That would be an aspect they share. There are also other sorts of properties brain events have in common that we wouldn't ordinarily think of as states or substates. These more abstract uniformities and similarities are often comfortably called "aspects."

I believe all of the things I have to say in this book can be said without much regimentation of this state and aspect talk. That is, I don't think the arguments for dualism depend on ontological subtleties that this flexibility is likely to mask, nor do I think my criticisms of those arguments depend on such subtleties. So sometimes I'll say that the subjective characters are states of the person, sometimes that they are states of the brain, and sometimes that they are aspects of brain states, depending on what seems to fit in a certain context. I should emphasize, however, that I focus on *types*. When I talk about pain, I am talking about a certain sensation that I have often had and others have too. I take it that each episode of pain is identical with a physical episode, but my view is also that each type of pain is identical with some physical state, and I am defending the coherence and adequacy of such a view.

2.4   The Metaphysics of Mental States

Experiences and thoughts are inner causes and effects.   Our commonsense view of mental states holds that they are states that are in some sense inside of us. They are directly caused by and directly cause other events inside of us; they are indirectly caused by and indirectly cause events outside of us. For example, my perception of an apple is caused by events in my eyes and optic nerve, themselves caused by external light and apples. This perception, in turn, may cause me, in conjunction with my hunger, to form an intention to reach out and grab the apple, with the eventual result that the apple is removed from the tree and eaten.

We need not beg the question against dualism to say this. Descartes himself thought that the point of causal interaction of the mind with the body was inside the head. We are rejecting certain theoretical alternatives, however. This bit of common sense does rule out the idea that mental states could simply be bits of behavior; they are rather the internal *causes* of behavior.

I think that it is common sense that mental states cause things and are caused by things in the same very general sense, that, say, the states of a computer or an automobile engine cause and are caused by other states of the computer or the engine. This is not to say that there aren't special things about mental states; in particular some of them provide reasons for action as well as causing action (see Israel, Perry, and Tutiya 1993). But whatever else they are, mental states are causes in the ordinary sense. We try to prevent other things from occurring by preventing the mental states that would cause them: I try not to make Elwood angry, so he won't shout at me, or hit me, or chew up my rug. We try to cause other things to occur by causing mental events to occur. The bank sends me a letter, telling me what they will do if I don't pay my loan. They are trying to cause money to arrive in the mail, by causing me to send it, by causing me to fear the consequences if I don't. Mental events are implicated as causes and effects in a huge percentage of the causal chains we worry about bringing about or preventing. When I turn the key, my plan for starting my car probably does not involve producing or preventing mental states, but the minute I start to drive in traffic, my planning needs to constantly take account of producing and preventing mental states in others, and so it will be for most of what I try to do for the rest of the day.

Further, we can say that many mental states have *typical* causes and effects, that is, causal roles. Some mental states have functions. What Chalmers calls psychological concept of mind makes perfectly good sense as part of the story of our concept of mind. We can have very rich concepts of our mental states as the states that have such and such causes, such and such effects, such and such cognitive functions, and so forth.

Experiences have subjective characters. But common sense also supports what Chalmers calls the phenomenal concept of mind. It holds that some of our mental states, which I'll call "experiences," have subjective characters in Nagel's sense. That is, experiences are those mental states that have the property that *it is like something to be in them*. What it is like to be in a brain state is its *subjective character*. These mental states include most centrally what we call sensations, including bodily sensations such as pain, thirst, and hunger, and sensations involved in external perception, such as the sensation of red I have when I look at a ripe tomato. It is also like something to have many emotions. It is like something to imagine and remember, in the sense of recalling events. I am assuming it is not always like something to have beliefs and be in other cognitive states, but thoughts are often attached to sensations and often involve images.

These subjective characters of brain states are probabilistically/nomically related to various other properties of brain states, have causal roles, and may have functions. But it is not part of common sense that they are *no more than* such causal roles or functions, and in fact is a pretty firm postulate of reflective common sense that they are more than that. There has been considerable debate on this point in recent philosophy. Block convincingly fights the battle for common sense with more diligence, engagement, imagination, and intelligence than I possess. Those who are seriously tempted by the idea that the properties of our brain states of which we are aware when we have an orgasm or taste a chocolate chip cookie are not only properties that have a causal role and serve some function, but simply *are* the properties of having that role or playing that function, should stop at this point and read "Mental Paint and Mental Latex" (Block 1995b) or its descendant "Mental Paint" (Block forthcoming). I will return to our example to drive home the point for the rest.

Consider the sort of pain that one feels when one accidentally hits one's own thumb with the hammer while vigor-
ously pounding a nail. Call the state one goes into when one
hits one's thumb in that way H. One could get into state H in
other ways, too, although probably by far the most common
way is the one I have described.

The state H then has a causal role, a certain syndrome of
typical causes and effects, to use David Lewis's terminology.
That is one aspect of H. And the state H also has a certain
subjective character. That is another aspect of state H. There
is no reason whatsoever apparent to common sense to suppose that the subjective character of H can be *identified* with
this other aspect, H's typical syndrome of causes and effects.
There is no reason that I can see that the physicalist should
think that this is so.

Some subjective characters are very important because they are
pleasant or unpleasant.   Some experiences are very pleasant and others are extremely unpleasant. This is a property
they have in virtue of their subjective characters. Seeking the
pleasant and avoiding the unpleasant is one of the keys to
animal and human motivation.

This division of subjective characters into the pleasant and
unpleasant is a very central fact about the architecture of the
animal mind. It is one way in which animal minds differ
from those of robots that have been built or that we have
presently have any conception of how to build. So subjective
characters really are quite important. I doubt very much that
a functional duplicate of a human being, or anything with
what Searle calls original or natural intentionality, could be
built that did not have pleasures and pains grounding the
intentional ascriptions.

Let's return to the pain I feel after I hit my thumb with
a hammer. My view is that this feeling is basically and

straightforwardly unpleasant. It's not unpleasant because
it delivers bad news about my thumb. It's not that I have
learned that it is bad to have bleeding, smashed thumbs,
and since this pain indicates to me that I have one of those, it
has become unpleasant to me. It is just unpleasant. If it were
the sensation I got from flossing my teeth, something that is
good for me, it would be just as unpleasant. As a matter of
fact the feelings I do have while flossing my teeth are not that
much fun, even though they signal to me that something
good is happening to my gums and thus provoke a pleasant thought. We seek to avoid unpleasant sensations and
are drawn to pleasant ones. We may put up with unpleasant ones because they are the sign of something beneficial
or avoid pleasant ones because they are the sign of something unhealthy. But the pleasantness or unpleasantness is
one thing, and what they signify is something quite different. This is not to deny that certain sensations and feelings
are pleasant or unpleasant for derivative reasons. Most of
the pleasantness and unpleasantness I experience during
the day may be of that sort. It may be hard to draw the
line. But whatever the source of pleasantness or unpleasantness, this fact about many sensations assures them a
prominent place in the causal order of human and animal
life.

For example, consider what it is like to chew up a chocolate chip cookie—that is, to be more specific, what it is like
to be in the brain states that are normally caused by chewing a fresh and warm-from-the-oven Mrs. Fields chocolate
chip cookie. These are very pleasurable states to be in. It is
possible that the pleasantness of those states is only deriva-
tively pleasurable, I suppose (without much conviction). But
at any rate, I've been in those states, and I'm now remembering them. These memories are caused in part by the states I

was in. And it is what it is like to have those memories, in the sense of vividly recalling the pleasure of eating such cookies, that causes me to pause when I see a Mrs. Fields cookie shop, to want to stop and to buy one, and to do so unless there are extremely strong reasons not to.

What it is like to be in the brain states that are typically caused by eating a high-quality chocolate chip cookie is quite unlike what it is like to be in the brain states typically caused by eating lima beans or brussels sprouts or, to take a rather dramatic case, chewing on zinc-coated nails. This last state is very unpleasant to be in for a person with the sort of fillings that chemically react to such nails, although perhaps not so bad as the one that one gets into when one hits one's thumb with a hammer.[3]

I dwell on these obvious facts to remind you of what we surely all believe pretheoretically: the experiences we have differ considerably in what they are like, and avoiding the unpleasant and seeking the pleasant experiences is one of the main motivations for deciding what to do.

Some subjective characters are very important because they carry crucial information.   When I hit my thumb with a hammer, the fact that my thumb is in pain carries the information that there is something wrong with my thumb. An event *e* carries the information that *P* (relative to some constraint and background) if *e* could not occur unless it was the case that *P* (assuming the constraints and background) (Israel and Perry 1990, 1991). Assuming the world works the way it normally does, sudden intense pain of that sort could not occur unless there was some damage to my thumb.

Of course, as Hume points out, pains are a pretty crude way to convey such information (Hume 1779). Having hit my own thumb and seeing it bleed and turn purple, the pain does not bring much news. It is rather like a BMW owner who sees someone back into his parked car and then hears his car alarm go off. The news value of the alarm does not justify its unpleasantness.

Our perceptual sensations provide us with information much more systematically and usually less painfully. That is, the nature of our visual, tactual, auditory, and other sensations provides us with information, relative to constraints and background assumptions. We are attuned to the informational value of changes in our sensations and adjust our thought and action to match. This is all quite independent of *attending* to the subjective character of these sensations and can be independent of even being aware of them (see below). I see the light turn red and slow down. The subjective character of my sensation changes, and I adjust to that change. The change in my subjective character is part of what it is to see the light turn red. And that change carries the information that the light I am looking at has turned red, which carries the conditional information that by not stopping I risk a ticket, an accident, or both.

Subjective characters are not external or historical aspects of inner states.   Our inner mental states have many properties, including their causal roles, their actual causes, their functions, and the like. The way our mental concepts work, the particular causes, effects, and other external factors about a thought or experience can partly determine its mentally relevant properties. Suppose, for example, I have a thought of the form I would express with "It is cold in here now" while sitting in Ventura Hall on Wednesday, December 5. This thought will have certain truth-conditions. It will be true only if it is cold in Ventura Hall at that time. The fact that the temperature in Ventura Hall is relevant to the truth of the thought, rather than the temperature in Cordura Hall, has to do with the fact that I am sitting in Ventura and not Cordura when I have the thought.

Or suppose I have a memory of a person entering Cordura Hall earlier in the day. It was only a quick glimpse. I think the person was Julius Moravcsik and infer that there is a philosopher in Cordura. At some point I hear about a conceptual emergency in Cordura, but I don't worry, because I think there is a philosopher on site. But in fact the person I saw was not the tall, happy philosopher Julius Moravcsik but the tall, happy linguist Dan Flickinger. Cordura will be in good shape for syntactic crises but not for conceptual ones. The thought I started with, "That man was Julius," was false, because the part of the thought expressed here with "that man" did not refer to Julius but to Dan Flickinger, because he was the person the perception was of that led to the memory. So here is a historical fact about my thought, having to do with something outside of my head at the time of the perception, that is relevant to its current properties, its content and its truth-value. Properties that are sensitive to contextual and historical factors are very important aspects of mental states that we use to classify and evaluate them for all sorts of purposes.

It seems clear, however, that the subjective character of a mental state is not a historical or contextual property of it. It is a property of it that is determined by current inner events. The phenomenal event will typically have external causes and effects, and it may have many current properties that are determined by such external factors. But the subjective character of the event will not be one of these properties. The subjective character is a matter of what it's like to be in the state, not its typical causes, nor its causes on a given occasion (see Block 1995b, forthcoming).

3   Thoughts about Sensations

Now I turn to some truths about how we think about and know about the subjective characters of our mental states. Again, I am not trying to provide a comprehensive theory, but to remind the reader of some fairly obvious facts and draw some perhaps not so obvious conclusions. Again, my arguments will not depend on my quaint terminology and simple-minded metaphors but should survive translation into more sophisticated approaches. My approach is intended to be largely in the spirit of two seminal articles advocating the two-ways strategy, one by Brian Loar (1990) and the other by William Lycan (1990).

In section 3.1, I make the very basic distinction between having experiences and knowing about them. Then, in section 3.2, given this basic distinction, I put our knowledge of experiences in the context of a general account of how we use ideas, notions, and concepts to keep track of things. In section 3.3 I take the step of identifying subjective characters and brain states, and in the last section I consider three doctrines I think physicalism must avoid.

3.1 Having and Knowing

When I hit my thumb with a hammer, I was in pain. I can also say that I felt pain. This suggests an analogy with the sense of touch. I reached for the apple, I felt it, I grasped it, I plucked it from the tree. It is a misleading suggestion. Having a pain is not perceiving a pain with the sense of touch, nor is it perceiving it in any way.

In the general case, it is not like something to be in relation to a certain object or event, unless we in some way perceive it. It is not like something to stand in front of the Mona Lisa; it is like something to see the Mona Lisa. It is not like something simply to have chocolate chip cookie in your mouth; it is like something to taste the chocolate chip cookie in your mouth. To say it is like something to be in a certain relation to an object means that typically being in that relation to the object causes us to have sensations involved in the perception of the object, and it is like something to have those.

But it would be a mistake to transfer this generalization to the sensations themselves. It is not like something to be in pain, or to have a sensation of red, or to taste a chocolate chip cookie, because we *perceive* those sensations. It is simply like something to be in those states. One may say that it is somewhat amazing and mysterious that it can be like something to be in a state. That is correct, but however amazing it may be, it is true. We gain nothing by pushing the mystery somewhere else in the mind. The states of our body, often carrying information about the external world, put our brains in states it is like something to be in. Amazing, but true. The mystery of sentience does not come when we perceive those states, or think about them, or know them; it comes when we are in them.

But of course we not only are in these states; we think about them, know about them, remember them, anticipate them, classify them, try to prevent some of them and to bring others about. We talk about them, as we are doing right now. The way we talk about them suggests that something like perception of them is involved. There are certainly basic dissimilarities with perception, the chief one being the one we just mentioned, that we do not know of our sensations *via* sensations they cause in us. There are no organs (like eyes, ears, or fingers) and there is no medium (like light or air).

But there are also similarities. We can be aware of our experiences. We can attend to their subjective characters. We can pay more or less attention to them. We can mentally demonstrate them ("This sensation . . . "), and communicate facts about them to others. We can notice what they are like, think about what they are like, remember what they are like, and anticipate what they will be like. We can form concepts of them and develop theories about them. In all these ways our knowledge of sensations is similar to knowledge of things we perceive.

I shall not say that we perceive our experiences (except via an autocerebroscope). But I shall assume that we have a variety of epistemic relations to them. We can be aware of them, attend to them, focus on them, note things about them, have concepts of them, have memory images of what it was like to be in them, and so forth.

I will say that an object (particular or universal) is *epistemically accessible* to you if it is in some relation that enables you to know about it. Most objects, whether particulars or universals, are accessible to you only if you are at the end of some sort of causal chain that carries information about them and leaves a trace on you. You perceive them, or read about them, or hear about them. Perhaps you pay no attention, but you are in a position to have knowledge. We can also know about objects that are causally downstream from our minds, that are going to be created or modified in accord with our intentions, desires, and the like.

From what we have said above, the conclusion is then unavoidable that the case with our own experiences is quite different. *Having* an experience, that is, merely being in a state that has a subjective character, makes the experience epistemically accessible to us. But this is not because it is causally upstream from our sensations or causally downstream from our intentions.

Feigl calls the relation our own experiences have to us, in virtue of which we can know about them, "acquaintance." Acquaintance itself is not knowledge. He distinguishes it sharply from knowledge *by* acquaintance; that is what you get by paying attention to and thinking about the experiences with which you are acquainted. I won't adopt the history-laden term "acquaintance." But I think the distinction is exactly right. We have experiences, and it is like something to have them. To have them is not to know anything about them or think about them or be conscious of them or be aware of them. It is simply to have them. But having them puts us in a position to attend to them, be aware of them, think about them, know things about them, form concepts of them, and so forth. Our experiences are epistemically accessible to us.

It seems quite plausible to me that many animals have experiences without knowing about them. They are sentient; they seek to get out of painful situations and stay in pleasant ones. But they do not attend to, theorize about, form concepts of, or talk about their experiences or distinguish them in any way from aspects of their situation that have to do with the states of external things rather than the states of themselves.

Humans, we might think, are always aware of their experiences; not only are experiences epistemically accessible for us, but we know of them in some way; we are at the very least aware of them. This view does not strike me as correct, even for humans. In the case of an adult human in a contemplative mood, say someone working on a philosophy essay, it is hard to imagine having an experience with a distinctive subjective character without being aware of it. But in fact this happens all the time. Right now I am refocusing on the feelings I have as my fingers hit the keys—something I don't usually do. I notice that my left forefinger is just slightly more sensitive than the others, perhaps even a bit sore. This act of attending to the experience is quite different than the experience itself. I've been having these experiences all along, but just now began attending to them, in order to find a good example of a hitherto unattended-to experience.

It is often the state of being aware of or knowing about an experience that is causally crucial to subsequent events. As I continue to focus on my left forefinger, I begin to worry. Perhaps that feeling is an early sign of repetitive stress injury. Perhaps I have some kind of tissue rot that is going to start with my left forefinger and quickly spread throughout my body. Perhaps this is the result of cracking my knuckles, and for that reason insurance won't cover it. And so forth. The sensation in my finger is really very minor and transitory and wouldn't have caused a problem at all if I hadn't noticed it while searching for hitherto unattended-to sensations. But the awareness of it has led to a whole series of further mental events, worries, fears, indignation (at the insurance company) and the like. I am so wrought up I may have to quit for the day.

3.2   The Epistemology of Experience

I assume that our minds, whatever else they may be or may do, provide us with a way of keeping track of things. We pick up information about things through perception; we store the information, draw inferences, speculate, anticipate, plan, and the like, as well as imagine and fantasize, the capacities for which may not be required to keep track of things but simply are certainly a nice dividend we are provided in virtue of having the necessary capacities. I assume our minds incorporate some system of representation, and that at least at some level of description and some level of understanding, it has the features exemplified by every system for keeping track of things that we understand how to design and build. So I assume a structured system of representations of things, places, properties, and the like, which become associated with one another in various ways to form thoughts, beliefs, desires, and so forth. The individual representations I call *ideas*. Those for individuals like you and me and Cincinnati I call *notions*. Those for universals of various sorts, such as properties and relations, I call *concepts*. I prefer this quaint, eighteenth-century terminology to the "language of thought" terminology because it helps me to keep in mind the important differences between thought and language, and in particular that the structure of the latter is shaped by the needs of communication whereas the former is shaped by the need for picking up, organizing, processing, and using information. Also these old-fashioned terms help remind me how crude my understanding of the structure of mental representations is. Finally, I like to pretend I'm writing in the eighteenth century, for it seems to have been a nice time to have been a philosopher, except for the plumbing and salaries.

To avoid thinking of ideas as words or images and to help remind myself that they are particulars, I like to think of them as manila file folders, full of heterogeneous kinds of information. This is a helpful metaphor. For one thing, it emphasizes the particularity of ideas, which in turn helps to keep the issue of analyticity in the background. Although we classify ideas by content for many purposes, we do not individuate them by content. The content of an idea can change.

The file folder metaphor also helps us appreciate that who or what an idea is *of* is determined not by content, but by circumstance. A student comes into my office and declares philosophy as her major. I pull out a file folder. I take some notes and dump them in, put her name on the tab, put her name on some forms to keep track of classes she has taken and dump them in, and so forth. Perhaps, if I'm a truly dedicated advisor, I take a Polaroid picture to help me recognize her when she returns. The file is of her because of the circumstances in which it was pulled out of the pile of new manila folders and given a use. The various things in it are of her or about her for a variety of reasons: the photo because it was taken of her, the transcript because it was xeroxed from one that was about her, my notes because they are from a conversation with her. With luck, all of the statements in the folder about her will be true and all the images accurate and will collectively distinguish her from everyone else in the world and allow me to recognize her again. But even if they don't, it is a file of her.

A file folder can have four quite distinct relations to an object. The object may be the original source or *origin* of the file, the object that led to the creation and use of the file in the first place. The student who came in my office was the *origin* of the file I created. She was also the *dominant source* of the information in the folder (Evans 1973). That is, the things I wrote in the file and put in the file were of her or about her. She was *denoted* by the content of the file folder. That is, she is included in the extension the properties attributed to the person the folder is of. Finally, she is the *applicandum*[4] of the file. That is, she is the person I'll apply it to; I'll use the file folder to guide my behavior toward her. When she comes back to see me I'll pull out that file folder and use the information in it to decide what to ask her, what to remind her she needs to take to graduate, and so forth.

If we conceive of ideas as abstract objects, defined by the properties they attribute, we will have little choice but to suppose that they are *of* the individuals or universals that have those properties. But this is simply not very plausible. We often have inaccurate concepts and incomplete notions of things and universals. If we take concepts to be particular (albeit complex and distributed) structures in the brain, we are not forced to take this implausible route. A much more plausible theory takes the default and paradigm to be that a concept is of its origin. Whether ordinary file or mental file, we expect the origin to be the dominant source of information, to be the applicandum, and to fit the concept reasonably well, well enough for the file to be useful. When these expectations are not met, the default can be overridden. I may apply the student's file to someone who looks like her and ask stupid questions. I may get grade sheets and other bits of information for which she isn't the source and mistakenly put them in her folder. There may be inaccurate information in the folder, so it no longer denotes her. Analogues to all of these things can and do happen with our mental files. Sometimes it is clear how to override the default. If the dominant source is not the origin (as in Evans' Madagascar case), the con-

cept can be usurped. Sometimes things become so confused that there is no clear answer to what or who the file
is of.

When it comes to forming a picture or battery of metaphors for how our minds handle relations, the file folder
analogy begins to limp badly, and something along the lines
of relational database theory would work better. For this
book, that won't be an issue, so I'll stick with the file folder
metaphor.

We have concepts of our experiences.   Our concepts of properties can contain all sorts of things: particular objects that
have the property, the typical causes of objects having the
property, the typical effects of having it, criteria for recognizing occurrences of the property, memory images of objects
that have the property, names of the property, and so forth.
What sorts of things we find will depend on what sorts of
properties the concepts are of and also on how they fit into
our own lives.

The things I've said about subjective characters have illus-
trated the sorts of things that can be parts of our concepts of
subjective characters. I have a concept of what it is like to
taste a good chocolate chip cookie. Unfortunately, as I write,
that concept is not attached to a present sensation of that
sort. It contains memory images, images of the cause (chocolate chip cookies), the effects (torpor, obesity), and so forth.
The idea finds its place in representations I have of various
facts and other states of affairs; my memories of past chocolate chip cookie eatings, my desires for and now developing
anticipations of future ones, and so forth.

Pain, of course, is not a single concept but a structure of
concepts concerning different sorts of pain. What I know
and believe about the cause of pain plays an enormously

important role in my life; I try to avoid having it and avoid causing it in others.

Although there is seldom a sharp analytic/synthetic distinction to be drawn in the case of our concepts, there are clearly things that are more and less central. When I was young I believed that headaches were caused by events inside the brain, where the problem seemed to be located. Perhaps there were not really little animals gnawing away, but something along those lines seemed to be going on. I gave up that belief, without changing my concepts of pain and headache significantly. The fact that headaches hurt is much more central, to put it mildly. In the case of our concepts of experiences, it seems that the most central parts, at least in many cases, will have to do with what the experience has been and will be like for us, the possessor of the concept.

Our concepts of sensations can include a variety of things, and like any of our concepts, can include various things at various times. As I mentioned above, there is often one sort of concept that seems most central and direct, however, and that is the sort of concept one has when one is having the sensation and attending to it. When Ewing wanted us to really get straight about pain, he didn't suggest remembering it or anticipating it. He didn't suggest reading an encyclopedia article about it. He suggested picking up a red-hot iron and *having* it. As one has it, one attends to it and thinks of it as "that$_i$ sensation" (where "that$_i$" is intended to suggest the sort of thinking one does while attending to aspects of one's inner life). What more direct, more clear and distinct concept could one have of pain than one that involves the attention to the very having of pain?

But of course we have a concept of pain when we are not in pain. A normal concept of pain, however, would be what I call *demonstrative/recognitional*; the concept has been formed by having pain, it includes a Humean memory of what it is like to have it, and these suffice to recognize when one is in pain.

There are self-directed methods of knowing the subjective character of one's experiences. There are various ways of knowing that one has a discoloration in the middle of one's back. One can be told by a mate, or a stranger at the beach, or a physician, for example. These people will know by looking, and that is the most direct way of knowing about discolorations on backs. There are also special, self-directed ways of looking at one's own back—that is, methods that work for most people to enable them to look at their own back but are usually neither necessary nor particularly good for looking at other peoples' backs. Some of us can stand with our backsides to a mirror, hold another mirror to catch the reflection of the first, and look at the second mirror. More flexible people can get by with one mirror, and the truly flexible can twist and see their own back without using a mirror at all. We don't usually think of these methods as "subjective." They employ the usual senses for finding out about external objects and don't differ in any dramatic way from the way others obtain the same information about us. Finding out about discolorations on my own back is pretty much like finding out about discolorations on the backs of others, it just requires more flexibility or more mirrors.

In the case of knowing what experiences we are having, we have not only self-directed methods but methods that are truly subjective. They are available only to the subject and are quite unlike methods available to others. The flow of information from the experience to the knowledge of it seems to be wholly contained within the confines of the subject's body. (Even to talk of "methods" or "ways" of knowing suggests some sort of recipe or set of criteria, which gives the wrong picture in many cases of knowledge of one's own experiences. I'll continue to use these words, but I hereby cancel any suggestion that the methods or ways in question involve step by step analysis or lists of criteria.) I can tell you if the experience I have is like the one I sought to have by eating a chocolate chip cookie. I just sort of notice. I don't need mirrors, and I don't need to twist and turn. It isn't just a matter of noticing what I put in my mouth. I may expect a quality chocolate chip experience, on the basis of the look and feel and origin of the cookie I put in my mouth, but be surprised. It tastes like an old turnip for some reason. I may expect not to have the real chocolate chip cookie experience—perhaps I have just been given something from the diet section of the supermarket, made without chocolate, butter, sugar, or eggs—but I may be quite pleasantly surprised. The method is just to chew and notice what it tastes like—although of course the connoisseur will cleanse the palate first. Methods of this sort I'll call "subjective." So there are self-directed but not subjective methods for finding out if one has a discoloration on one's back and self-directed, subjective methods for finding out if one is having the experience characteristic of eating high-quality chocolate chip cookies, or is in pain, or is seeing red, or is rotating an image in one's mind, or is telling oneself to keep one's left arm straight and feet planted firm and follow through.

There are also plenty of other-directed methods for finding out about experiences others are having. We use the evidence of bodily condition, behavior, and testimony in the context of an assumption of physical similarity. These methods can be very secure and can override apparently sincere testimony on the part of the person having the experiences. I am very confident that I know what my grandchild is feeling

about an hour after finishing his soda, as he squirms and fid-
gets. I take him to the bathroom, in spite of his protests. My
inference is based on when and how much he last drank. The
inference is not only about the state of his bladder but also
about what he is feeling. I want him to learn to associate the
feeling he is having, and is capable of being aware of, attending to, and properly classifying, with the necessity of a trip
to the bathroom.

As I mentioned at the outset of the book, I think it is conceivable for me to be aware of my grandchild's experience,
in as direct a way as it is open to me to be aware of any com-
parably small and well-protected physical phenomenon.
The brain is behind a skull; the aspects of the brain in question may be subtle and complex and involve various non-
contiguous parts. Finding the aspects of the brain of which
one is subjectively aware would not be simple, even if we
could shrink me along with Raquel Welch and her team and
inject them into my grandchild's brain. Still, as I use the
term, the force of "subjective" is not to deny to others the
possibility of awareness of an event in one's person but to
affirm that there are special methods available to the subject. There are methods for knowing about experiences that
can be applied only when one has the experience, by the person that has it, and that are direct in at least the sense of not
involving the organs and media of external perception.

*Remembering and anticipating sensations is, in some bewildering
way, like having them.*   It does not hurt to remember the last
time I hit my thumb with a hammer, nor does it hurt to anticipate the next time. But the memory and the anticipation
are rather unpleasant. There is some uncanny *likeness*, something Hume was right about with his quaint thought that
ideas resembled impressions. When I remember headaches,

my brow furrows. When I remember the fall I took on my left shoulder, I find myself rubbing it. When I remember eating a chocolate chip cookie, my tongue starts to move around my mouth and a little sense of emptiness develops in my stomach.

There is a sense of fit when I have a sensation of a type I remember having before. It is hard to say much about this, but it is quite unlike some other cases of identification and recognition. There is not a checklist of criteria. It's more like comparing a color chip with a painted surface—but it's not really very much like that.

The bottom line is simply that by attending to our experiences, we often gain the ability to recognize them and have more or less vivid memories and anticipations of them that involve some kind of imagery. These images and the abilities to call them up become parts of our concepts of the experiences in question. The extent to which we can do this varies considerably with different types and modalities of experience. I'll call the parts of our concept of subjective states that are based on being in them, knowing of them in special subjective ways, and imagistically anticipating and remembering them the "Humean core" of these concepts or the "Humean idea" included in them.

The Humean cores of our concepts of sensations are likely to be central.   That is a wordy way of saying that the most central part of my concept "pain in my left hand" is "something that feels like *this*," where I attend to a memory of having a pain in my left hand or, if I am truly devoted to philosophy, attend to the pain I feel in my left hand when I pick up Ewing's iron rod. Anything like this would be "pain in my left hand" even if it were not caused by damage to my left hand (Joe DiMaggio had pain in his toe caused by a damaged tooth—at any

rate, so we once were told). *This* sort of thing (remembering a headache) is a headache. You *may* convince me that
they are caused by misalignments of skull plates, rather than
brain rats. Whatever the cause, a headache is a headache. But
headaches have got to feel like *this*, and anything that does
is a headache.

Not every concept of a subjective character will have this
"demonstrative/recognitional" structure, with memories of
one's own experiences and recognitional abilities as central.
A red-green color-blind person may think that *the* subjective
character of seeing red objects, the experience people generally have, is *not* the one he has when he sees red objects.
A blind person who has never been sighted or has no relatively vivid memories from when he was sighted of seeing
a puce object and has had no nonperceptual color experiences that involved knowingly experiencing the subjective
character of seeing puce will presumably have no positive
subjective core to his concept of the sensation of seeing puce.
However, neither do I for that matter, since I can never remember what puce things look like. I don't know what it's
like to see puce, although I could find out. I don't know what
it's like to navigate the way bats do, and I don't know how
to find out—I can't even imagine.

We take subjective characters to be real kinds, projectable onto
other kinds in the natural world.   Suppose now I accidentally
put a zinc-coated nail in my mouth for the first time. I have
a very unpleasant sensation, which I am aware of and take
to be caused by the zinc-coated nail. I not only spit out the
nail, I resolve to avoid such sensations in the future, by never
again putting zinc-coated nails in my mouth. My reasoning,
if made explicit, seems to amount to something like this:
"*This* kind of sensation is extremely unpleasant. I am having

this kind of sensation because I put a zinc-coated nail in my mouth. Best not to do that again."

I think according to common sense this is a pretty reasonable way to think. We would think that someone was quite mad who repeatedly put zinc-covered nails in her mouth in spite of finding the sensation thus produced most unpleasant. So the idea that sensations have a certain aspect that makes them pleasant or unpleasant to have, and that that aspect is one we can attend to using self-directed methods and also one that is caused by certain larger situations, which we can avoid putting ourselves in, is quite congenial to common sense. Subjective characters are real kinds that "project onto" other physical kinds in ways that make it possible, to a certain extent, to anticipate and control them.

Although there may be a certain amount of indeterminacy about which state we are attending to, there are some clear facts of the matter. Suppose that I am looking at a tree of a certain kind—an elm, say. I utter the words "That kind of tree used to be found all over Nebraska." To what do the words "that kind of tree" refer? The matter is to a certain extent indeterminate. If we take the phrase to refer to the kind, *elm*, then my remark is true, for at one time, before the spread of Dutch elm disease across America's Great Plains in the 1950s and 1960s, Nebraska had many elms. But perhaps the tree I am looking at is a new disease-resistant subspecies of elm that did not exist in the 1950s and 1960s. Then we could take the phrase to refer to the subspecies, in which case my remark would be false. It may be that more details about the example would count decisively in favor of one interpretation or another, but in many cases it is surely indeterminate.

Consider the kind *trees that look similar to this one.* It seems I might be referring to this kind of tree, that is, a large, deciduous shade-providing tree with small leaves and an umbrella-like branch structure. This kind might include many kinds of elms but not all and some kinds other than elms. If a tree-loving person who did not know much about trees said, looking at a classically shaped elm, "I want a tree of that kind in my yard," this is probably the kind she is referring to.

A couple of negative facts about reference seem quite clear. In these cases I am not referring to the kind or class of trees that are seen by me, either those that are seen at the time of the remark or those that have *ever* been seen by me. One may doubt that this class of trees even constitutes a kind, at least in the more restrictive senses of "kind." I am referring to the kind I refer to, in virtue of looking at a tree of that kind. But I am not referring to the "kind" *looked at by me*.

As in the case of elms, there is a certain indeterminacy in our reference to experiences. There may be a whole hierarchy of unpleasant sensations, of which the one caused by putting a zinc-coated nail in one's mouth is a particular subspecies, many members of which one could take my thought and resolve to be about. But as with the case of elms, there are certain pretty clear facts of the matter.

Let's name the kind of sensation that chewing on zinc-coated nails in fact causes Z. This very sensation could be caused by something else, say, chewing on warm chocolate chip cookies, if our world worked differently than it does. There is no logical contradiction in its working that way. If we are thinking about a possible world or counterfactual circumstance in which this is so, then we need to distinguish between the kind of sensation caused in that circumstance by chewing on zinc-coated nails and Z. When I resolve to avoid *this sensation*, focusing on the sensation I am having as I chew the zinc covered nails, it is Z that I am resolving to avoid. Possible worlds that work differently—in which I avoid chewing on zinc-covered nails, and in which I never have the sensation that so chewing causes in those worlds, but I *do* have Z—do not fit my resolve. Worlds in which zinc-covered nails taste like chocolate chip cookies, and in which I chew on them all the time, but I never have Z, do fit my resolve.

To put this another way: My resolve not to chew zinc-covered nails is *derivative* from my resolve to avoid having Z. If the link between them were to be broken, or if I were to find out that it did not exist in the first place—perhaps some bug spray had gotten on these nails and was the real cause of Z—I would stick with the resolve to avoid Z, but might occasionally pop some zinc-coated nails in my mouth when it was convenient to do so. There may be some indeterminacy about what state I am referring to, especially in the context of a fine-grained system of scientific classification, that would probably find at least as many unpleasant sensations involved with zinc-coated nails as there are species of elm. But some things are clear.

3.3   Mental States as Physical States

So far there is nothing contrary to neo-dualism in antecedent physicalism. Our commonsense view recognizes subjective characters. It has not pronounced them physical or not. This is an acknowledgment that common sense is, as Smart puts it, "topic-neutral" about mental states (Smart 1959). Our strategy is, in a sense, a return to Smart's idea that our commonsense concepts of our mental states do not say what kind of states they are; they could be states of brain or states of the heart, chemical states or electrical states or even nonphysical states, if the concept of nonphysical states is otherwise coherent. Our mental concepts are not completely neutral. I think common sense and philosophical considerations can rule out at least crude forms of logical behaviorism, for example. And our mental concepts evolve and reflect common knowledge, which now includes that the brain is crucial to the continuation of mental life.

One path from Smart's insight has been very well traveled. One way for a concept to be topic-neutral is for it to consist of a partial description of the item of which it is a concept. We don't need the whole truth about a thing or a property to have a descriptive concept of it. I may have the concept of Natasha's teacher and have quite a few opinions about this person without knowing whether the teacher is male or female, over or under forty, a native Californian or a transplant, a Republican or a Democrat, and so forth. My concept is partial; on the issues on which it is silent, it is neutral. It is a gender-neutral, age-neutral, home-state-neutral, and politically neutral concept of Natasha's teacher.

The well-traveled road is that our concepts of mental states are neutral because they are theoretical-descriptive concepts. The concepts for which this is right are the ones Chalmers calls "psychological" as opposed to phenomenal. The idea is that mental states are the states that occupy a given causal or functional role provided by "folk psychology." This is *one* way of supplying the details for the partial description version of the topic-neutral strategy. It sees mental-state concepts as descriptive and theoretical. Mental-state concepts can be neutral because they are roughly of the form "The typical cause of so-and-so and the typical effect of such-and-such, whatever it may be." The concept that we grasp when we learn folk psychology or commonsense psychology is partial. It says that mental states are causes and effects, but it does not specify that they are brain states or even physical states.

Providing a theoretical-descriptive account is not, however, the only way of following the topic-neutral strategy. A second way is providing an ostensive or *demonstrative* account (Loar 1990). I may see Natasha's teacher on the playground when I attend Grandparents' Day at her school. I have a concept of *that person*. Like all concepts, it has a descriptive element. It is not theoretical-descriptive but rather demonstrative-descriptive. And it is partial. I see Natasha's teacher and still do not know a lot about him or her. The age, the educational philosophy, the marital status, the home state, even the gender may not be apparent. Just as I may have a very indeterminate and neutral idea what sort of object plays a certain causal role called for in a theory, I may have a very neutral and indeterminate idea what sort of object I am ostensively or demonstratively aware of.

Given our epistemology of phenomenal states, it is this ostensive strategy we shall pursue. At the heart of our concepts of phenomenal states, especially the most dramatic and familiar ones like pain and color sensations, are demonstrative-recognitional concepts. We suppose that our concepts of subjective characters are topic-neutral. Or more carefully, we assume that our concepts of subjective characters can be made topic-neutral through philosophical reflection without abandoning their core. We can retain the nonfunctionalist core of our concepts, the idea that being like *this* is what makes a pain a pain, a sensation of red a sensation of red, and so forth, even while we accept that the reference of *this* is a physical aspect of a brain state.

The move from mere common sense to antecedent physicalism consists, then, of supposing that the subjective characters of our experiences are physical states of the brain. This is a supposition of an identity between types or kinds of events. The first is a type of event we are aware of when we have an experience and perhaps make resolutions to avoid it, like our kind Z in the last section. The second is a physical type, of the sort that can be in theory physically observed, say by Leibniz's men in an enlarged brain, or the shrunken people of *Fantastic Voyage*, or more reasonably, by complex scientific methods of brain observation involving various kinds if instruments for detecting and representing events that are typically hidden by skulls and tissue and are also very small. That is our hypothesis going into the neo-dualist arguments. It is not a piece of dogma but an antecedently plausible or at least attractive hypothesis. Our job is to see if the neo-dualist arguments give us a reason to abandon it. Before going on to a couple of doctrines that antecedent physicalism does not include, let's make sure we understand clearly what it does support, by looking at one more version of the experience gap argument.

It is common sense to distinguish between the event of putting nails into my mouth and chewing them and the unpleasant sensation that this rather stupid move caused. There is a gap between the two, the gap of cause and effect. As we go along the causal path from teeth, tongue, mouth, and nails to brain, we will want to make similar distinctions. One could perhaps create episodes of virtual zinc-covered nail biting, using computers and little electrodes connected to the nerves that would be discharged if one were one chewing on zinc-coated nails. Or one could bypass the nerves that go from mouth to brain and intervene with electrodes and such at the periphery of the brain. And so forth. At each point we would want to distinguish between the cause and the effect—that is, the unpleasant experience and what causes it.

One might want to infer from this, using some kind of misguided induction, that we will *never* reach any physical state that may simply *be* the subjective character caused by chewing the zinc-coated nails, as opposed to being yet another cause of it, further along the causal path. The qualia, on this picture, elude capture within the physical system. We will return to this idea later; the point I make now is that there is no reason, following from antecedent physicalism as I have presented it, to accept that qualia are elusive in this way.

The picture the antecedent physicalist has is much more simpleminded, for better or worse. Consider the ringing of a telephone. It is typically caused by someone calling us, but not always. There are wrong numbers, and there are glitches in the line. We could identify various other events sufficient for the ringing along the line: events at the pole, events at the point where the wire connects to the house, events in the wiring inside the house, events at the interface between the phone and the wire from the wall, events inside the phone on the way to the clapper and bell. But when we get to the clapper and the bell, we are there. The clapper repeatedly hitting the bell *is* the ringing of the phone.

We can imagine a whole nested set of events that are what the world is typically *like* when a phone rings: the caller calling, the wires buzzing, the phone innards reacting, the clapper hitting the bell. Then we can pare off the outer layers. There is what goes on *in the outside wires, the house wires, the phone, and the bell* when the phone rings. Pare off the outside world, and there is still what goes on *in the house wires, the phone, and the bell* when the phone rings. Pare off what happens between the point where the wires enter the house and the phone, and there is still what goes on *in the phone and the bell* when the phone rings. And finally pare off the rest of the phone so all we have is what goes on *with the bell* when the phone rings. But this last event differs from the rest. There is no more cause left, just effect: the ringing of the phone.

Similarly, we can ask what the world is like, what the environment is like, what the body as a whole is like, what the brain is like, and what some smaller and smaller parts of the brain are like when I have subjective character Z. On the antecedent physicalist view, at some point along this chain we will come to a part or parts of the brain being in a certain physical state or undergoing certain physical changes. We will have peeled off as much as we can of the whole complex event while leaving what is necessary for the sensation of chewing nails. This *is* what it is like in the relevant parts of the brain when one chews on zinc-covered nails. According to antecedent physicalism, this state of these parts of the brain *is* exactly what we are aware of subjectively when we think of "this state" and resolve never to be in it again.

3.4   Doctrines Physicalism Must Avoid

As we look at the arguments for dualism, what antecedent physicalism *doesn't* commit us to will be as important as what it *does* commit us to. I end this chapter by listing and very briefly explaining three doctrines to which physicalists are often thought to be committed. They are not doctrines that follow from the view put forward in this chapter. We will return to each of these doctrines in later chapters, as we discuss the neo-dualist arguments, for those arguments each turn on supposing that one or more of these doctrines is a necessary part of the physicalist point of view.

Epiphenomenalism

Epiphenomenalism is the view that mental states are caused but have no effects, or at least no physical effects. They make no difference to the physical world. They may appear to do so, since the things that cause the mental events also cause other physical events that will appear to be caused by the mental events. But this is an illusion. Mental events (or more accurately historically, the laws that link physical causes with mental effects) are "nomological dangers."

A restricted form of epiphenomenalism, given Chalmers' distinction, is that whatever may be the case for psychological mental events, the phenomenal events—the occurrences of subjective characters—have no effects and make no difference to the physical world.

There is no reason whatsoever for the antecedent physicalist to be an epiphenomenalist in either the broader or the narrower sense. Indeed the opposite, what Lewis calls "the efficacy of the mental," is a basic tenet of antecedent physicalism (Lewis 1966). Mental states, including phenomenal states, cause all sorts of physical events, and to think otherwise flies in the face of the common sense that is the basis of antecedent physicalism.

The Subject Matter Assumption

This view is a bit harder to state and a bit less obviously related to the issue of physicalism. When we consider the knowledge argument we will see, however, that it is quite important. Here is the basic idea. A bit of knowledge has a subject matter, the properties and objects that are known about. I know that Berlin is in Germany; the subject matter of this bit of knowledge is Berlin, Germany, and the relation of a city being in, or a part of, a nation. It is natural to identify the content of an episode of knowledge with what is known about the subject matter. If we do that, then quite different episodes of knowledge, involving different agents at different places and times and quite different relationships to the subject matter, can have exactly the same content. Someone can know exactly the same thing, even though he would express it, being a Berlin resident, with "Diese Stadt ist in Deutschland." This kind of content, then, does not *locate* the knower relative to the subject matter nor does it require any particular system of representation. The subject matter is not (at least typically) the knower or his ideas or words but the things they are ideas of or words for.

I'll argue in a later chapter that this picture gives a very distorted view of knowledge and leaves out an important aspect of knowledge that I'll call *reflexive content*. If we don't understand the reflexive content of episodes of knowledge, we will be at a loss to understand a number of important phenomena, such as recognizing and identifying things.

I'll claim that it is the subject matter principle, and not physicalism, that leads to the problem with Mary of the knowledge argument. It's not easy to say ahead of time why this should be so, so I'll just have to ask readers to wait and see, when we get to these topics in chapters 5, 6, and 7.

Functionalism and Supervenience

Some fairly persuasive arguments have been put forward to show that intentional states, such as belief and desire, are more likely to be functional states than more straight-forwardly physical states. The correct relation is not identity but "realization" and "supervenience."

Consider the type of object we call a "valve." A valve has a certain function; it allows a fluid to pass through when it is in one state and prevents it from passing through when it is in another state. There are a variety of ways of making things that can do this. Valves can have different designs, be made of different materials, and so forth. We shouldn't identify the property of being a valve with any one of these. Rather, the property of being a valve is *realized* by each way of making valves; being a valve is *multiply realized*. The state of being a valve is the state a thing is in when it is in some (first-order) state that fulfills the valve function. Being a valve is a physical state only in the sense that the physical composition and design of the thing will determine whether it is a valve or not; valvehood *supervenes* on physical properties.

It has been argued that, somewhat similarly, there may be many ways beliefs could be realized; that is, many ways of building a system for storing, processing, and applying information. For different kinds of agents—robots, Martians, and so on—quite different materials and designs might be needed. So the idea is that belief needs to be a functional, second-order state, something that is realized by, rather than identical with, straightforwardly physical states; one's states of belief supervene on one's physical states, rather than being identical with them.

Whatever the merits of these considerations for belief and other propositional attitudes, or for what Chalmers call *psychological* properties, they provide no motivation for thinking of the subjective characters of experiences as functional, second-order properties. We might become convinced, for example, that some extraterrestrials with a quite different basic chemistry than us had states that had subjective characters, were unpleasant for the extraterrestrials, led those who were in them to avoid similar situations in the future, and so forth. That would not provide us with a reason for supposing that what it was like to be in the various pain states of the extraterrestrials was what it was like to be in our pain states. If we drew that conclusion, then we could not hold that the subjective characters of our painful experiences are simply physical properties of physical states. The antecedent physicalist sees no reason to draw the conclusion.

4   The Zombie Argument

As the first step in his zombie argument, David Chalmers invites us to consider what he describes as a logical possibility:

[C]onsider the logical possibility of a *zombie*: someone or something physically identical to me (or to any other conscious being), but lacking conscious experiences altogether. At the global level, we can consider the logical possibility of a *zombie world*: a world physically identical to ours, but in which there are no conscious experiences at all. In such a world, everybody is a zombie.

So let us consider my zombie twin. This creature is molecule for molecule identical to me, and identical in all the low-level properties postulated by a completed physics, but he lacks conscious experience entirely. (Some might prefer to call a zombie "it," but I use the personal pronoun; I have grown quite fond of my zombie twin.) To fix ideas, we can imagine that right now I am gazing out the window, experiencing some nice green sensations from seeing the trees outside, having pleasant taste experiences through munching on a chocolate bar, and feeling a dull aching sensation in my right shoulder.

What is going on in my zombie twin? He is physically identical to me, and we may as well suppose that he is embedded in an identical environment. He will certainly be identical to me *functionally*: he will be processing internal configurations being modified appropriately and with indistinguishable behavior resulting. He will be *psychologically* identical to me. . . . He will be perceiving the trees outside, in the functional sense, and tasting the chocolate, in the psychological sense. All of this follows logically from the fact that he is physically identical to me, by virtue of the functional analyses of psychological notions. . . . It is just that none of this functioning will be accompanied by any real conscious experience. There will be no phenomenal feel. There is nothing it is like to be a zombie. (Chalmers 1996, 94–95)

According to the zombie argument, then, it is logically possible that there be a world in which people are exactly like us in every physical detail but do not have conscious experiences. These people would be indistinguishable from us in terms of behavior and physical structure down to the last detail.

4.1   Why Zombies Could Not Be Physically Like Us

I'll use the term "zombie world" for a possible world in which there is no consciousness but there are creatures that look and act like us and are like us inside, *insofar as this is possible given the lack of consciousness*. That is, a zombie world will be just like ours except for the conscious states *and whatever other differences the lack of conscious states implies*.

I'll use the term "Chalmers zombie world" for a world that is a zombie world, and is, as Chalmers' argument requires, physically *indiscernible* from ours. (I'll also use the term "(almost) Chalmers zombie world" for a world that is a zombie world and is physically indiscernible from ours except for the absence of conscious events. (Almost) Chalmers zombie worlds won't enter the discussion until the next section, when the need for them will be explained.)

From the point of view of an antecedent physicalist, it seems that zombie worlds are possible, but Chalmers zombie worlds are not. The reason is that the antecedent physicalist believes in the efficacy of the conscious and rejects epiphenomenalism. Since the antecedent physicalist thinks that conscious mental states bring about changes in the world, it seems that a world without them will have to differ in some way from ours. Either the changes won't occur, or they will occur but will be caused by something else. If conscious states make a difference in the way our bodies work and ultimately in how we behave, and they are absent in the zombie world, then how could everything in the physical world be the same as it is in our world?

An analogy: We can imagine a world like ours but with no water. But we cannot imagine a world with no water and everything else the same. If there were no water, there would be no plant growth, no floods, and so forth and so on. We might imagine a world just like our world was on July 1, 1955, with all of the water suddenly or gradually removed. For some reason, let's suppose, the process of condensation ceases, although evaporation continues. As time passes, the lack of water in that world will cause it to diverge in more and more major ways from our world. The plants will die, the fish will die, the people will die, and so forth and so on. This would be true whether or not water was reducible to hydrogen and oxygen, or, contrary to fact, were a perfectly separate substance not further reducible. Still, if water plays a causal role, and you remove the water, everything else will not be the same.

If we removed the conscious states from our world, say just as it is right this minute, as we imagined doing with the water, what would happen? We leave all of the (other) physical states intact, and all the of the laws of nature intact, except those that have conscious states as effects. What will this world be like? If we believe in the principle of the efficacy of the conscious—that is, if we believe that in our world conscious states make a difference—then we will think that this zombie world will begin to diverge from ours. Consider the case of me picking up the red-hot piece of charcoal. In the zombie world I will not feel the pain, as I do in this one. So the things that that feeling of pain causes, such as memories of a certain sort, either will not occur or will occur for different causes. In either case, our world will have to be different from the zombie world.

To take a more pleasant example, suppose that I bite into a fresh, warm chocolate chip cookie. I am in the state of being somewhat hungry and, for some reason, not worried about my weight or other health matters. I taste the chocolate chip cookie in the phenomenal as well as the psychological sense. I attend to the what-it-is-like property of my brain state—although of course it seems very much like something wonderful happening in my mouth. I say, "Boy, was that good!" I find it simply incredible—not inconceivable, but really quite incredible—that the conscious event was not part of the cause of my saying what I did. It seems to me that if some other conscious event occurred, such as the kind of conscious event that occurs when one chews on zinc-coated nails, I would not have said what I did at all. And it seems to me that if no conscious events occurred when I chewed the cookie—if my stream of consciousness had just continued on, with no new taste sensations—I would have been surprised and disappointed and would not have said, "Boy, was that good!" So it seems to me that the conscious event was a cause of my remark, an INUS condition in John Mackie's terms: an *i*nsufficient but *n*ecessary part of an *u*nnecessary but *s*ufficient condition.

Let's now consider my zombie twin. We are asked to suppose that my zombie twin puts the cookie in his mouth, chews it up, and says, "Boy was that good!" But what will make him say that if there is no conscious state, no burst of chocolate chip cookie flavor in his mouth?

Of course, zombie-John might utter the sentence "Boy was that good!" The same observable events might happen in the zombie world as in the actual one. It might happen as a result of a different cause or simply occur with no cause at all. The antecedent physicalist can certainly suppose all of this to be logically possible, without in any way compromising the view that the conscious state is a physical state of the brain, for such a world will not be physically indiscernible from ours and hence not a Chalmers zombie world.

So we need to be careful of the difference between simply imagining a zombie world and imagining a Chalmers zombie world. Consider any specific event that we suppose is caused in part by a specific conscious state. Call the event X. Suppose X is caused by the combination of A, B, and C. A and B are the physical causes and C is a conscious state. Together they are a sufficient condition for the physical event X, and each is a necessary part of the sufficient condition. In the zombie world C, the conscious event, doesn't occur. So if the zombie world works just as ours does, X won't occur either, because the physical conditions, without C, are not sufficient. And so the zombie world isn't just like ours. But of course we can imagine X occurring in the zombie world, even though C doesn't occur. X can just occur. Why not? It could just occur sort of miraculously, or it could be that the physical principles of the zombie world are different than the actual world, so that A and B are causally sufficient for X. So again, the zombie world isn't physically just like ours. In our world, X occurs, caused by the combination of A, B, and C, and A and B alone are not physically sufficient for X.

I want to mention two possible misunderstandings. First, I am not claiming that we are always right about the effects of our conscious states. Suppose I perform Ewing's experiment, and pick up a piece of red-hot charcoal. I feel pain, I drop the charcoal. It seems to me that the feeling of pain caused me to drop the charcoal. I may wrong about that. It may well be that I drop the charcoal, quite independently of the feeling of pain; that the feeling of pain, and the release of the muscles that hold the charcoal, are both caused by more immediate effects of the heat of the charcoal on my nervous system, rather than the pain being the cause of the release, as it seems. There is no reason for the antecedent physicalist to think that we are always right about what conscious states cause.

But note that in a case like this, the feeling of pain will have other effects. The next time someone suggests that I pick up a piece of charcoal, for example, I will be very reluctant, because I remember what the pain was like. It would be very hard to accept that the memory of what it was like did not depend on what it was like and that the influence of the memory was not connected to the nature of the memory—to what it is like to vividly remember picking up the charcoal. It is very hard to accept that if the experience of picking up a piece of red-hot charcoal was like the experience of eating a warm chocolate chip cookie, I would not at least be tempted to perform the experiment again.

The second possible misunderstanding is this. It might seem that I am saying that a certain world isn't possible, for contingent reasons. That is, because antecedent physicalism happens to be true, a contingent fact, the Chalmers zombie world isn't possible. But what is possible should not depend on contingent facts.

Part of the answer to this objection will depend on issues about identity, necessity, and conceivability, which I'll consider in chapter 8. But the basic point is simply this. A

Chalmers zombie world is not simply a world in which various things occur. It is certainly possible that there be a world with all of the same events as ours except for the conscious events. That is not enough for it to be a Chalmers zombie world. The second condition a Chalmers zombie world has to meet is being physically indiscernible from ours. That is a matter of having a certain similarity to the world that happens to be actual. Whether a given possible world qualifies as a Chalmers zombie world, then, is not simply a matter of what happens in it but also a matter of its similarity to the actual world. So whether a given possible world qualifies as a Chalmers zombie world depends on contingent facts about the actual world, namely, what the actual world is like. The antecedent physicalist simply claims that none of the possible worlds meet both of the conditions of being a Chalmers zombie world. The point is not that if the causal facts are different, some world is not logically possible that otherwise would be. The point is that if those facts are different, that world, though logically possible, is not a Chalmers zombie world.

This is not too surprising. The antecedent physicalist supposes that the what-it-is-like properties *are* physical properties. So clearly the antecedent physicalist will find a problem in the claim that there is a logically possible world that is physically indiscernible from ours but in which no one has any what-it-is-like states.

4.2   Dualism and Epiphenomenalism

What may be somewhat surprising, though, is that the possibility of a Chalmers zombie world really has virtually nothing at all to do with the issue of physicalism versus dualism. It is a test for epiphenomenalism versus the efficacy of the

Table 4.1
Two Separate Issues

	Epiphenomenalism	Efficacy of the Conscious
Physicalism	Conscious states are physical nomological danglers, in principle publically observable	Antecedent physicalism
Dualism	Chalmers' position: Conscious states as nonphysical nomological danglers	Commonsense dualism: The physical world is not a closed system

conscious. The two issues are independent. Table 4.1 shows the various possibilities.

Epiphenomenalism is usually considered to be a form of dualism. But we defined it simply as the doctrine that conscious events are effects but not causes. So defined, it appears to be consistent with physicalism.[5] A physicalist epiphenomenalist cannot accept the possibility of the Chalmers zombie world, since if sensations are physical states, and we remove the sensations, things are not physically indiscernible. But he can accept the possibility of (almost) Chalmers zombie worlds, the ones that are physically indiscernible except for the absence of the sensations. The zombie argument does not provide an argument for dualism. As long as one is an epiphenomenalist, one can accept the possibility of zombies.

On the other hand, one can be a dualist and accept the efficacy of the conscious. Indeed, this may be unreflective common sense, and it has certainly been philosophical common sense throughout certain periods of history. It is natural to believe in the efficacy of the conscious, and, because of the intuitions captured by Ewing, dualism is natural too.

There is nothing inconsistent about this position. Its advocate would find the Chalmers zombie world quite impossible for exactly the same reasons the antecedent physicalist does. Since conscious events make a physical difference, a physical world without them cannot be physically indiscernible from our own. The problem with commonsense dualism is not inconsistency but that the arguments for it, however intuitive their force, are simply not compelling in the face of arguments against it. Against it, among other things, are the difficulty of saying much positive and testable about nonphysical properties and the wide acceptance of the hypothesis that the physical world is a closed system: that physical events have only physical causes.

All four entries in table 4.1, then, are occupied by logically consistent positions. My point has not been that Chalmers' view is impossible but only that the Chalmers zombie world is. Of course, *if* one is an epiphenomenalist, *then* it will not seem impossible that a world could be without conscious experiences and yet (otherwise) physically indiscernible from ours. But the acceptance of this possibility still does not provide an argument for dualism, for it should be as acceptable to the physicalist epiphenomenalist as the dualist epiphenomenalist.

The possibilities of zombies, then, seems to be a test for dividing epiphenomenalists from nonepiphenomenalists, not an argument for defending dualism against physicalism. All epiphenomenalists pass the test of finding Chalmers zombies conceivable, either exactly as Chalmers presents them or almost exactly; all nonepiphenomenalists fail it. Both dualists and physicalists pass the test if they are epiphenomenalists and fail it if they are not.

At most, then, the zombie argument is an argument for epiphenomenalism. But it is not a very convincing one. If there is a Chalmers zombie world or an (almost) Chalmers zombie world, then epiphenomenalism must be true. To show that there is a possible world meeting certain conditions, one must imagine or describe it in enough detail to be sure it is possible and meets the conditions in question. We can surely describe a zombie world, but to meet the conditions to be even an (almost) Chalmers zombie world it has to be physically indiscernible from the actual world, except for the absence of conscious events. What reason would we have to suppose that among the possible worlds meeting the conditions of being zombie worlds, there is one that meets the further condition of being an (almost) Chalmers zombie world? I cannot see any reason we would think this, unless we were *already* epiphenomenalists.

4.3   Supervenience and Epiphenomenalism

I've oversimplified Chalmers so far, in an important way, by leaving out the topic of supervenience. If we go back to the quote with which I opened the chapter, we find that the conditions on the zombie world seem to shift a bit from the first paragraph to the second. In the first he says the zombie world is "physically identical to ours," but in the second paragraph he says, "[L]et us consider my zombie twin. This creature is molecule for molecule identical to me, and identical in all the low-level properties postulated by a completed physics, but he lacks conscious experience entirely." So what is the zombie world supposed to be like? Is it physically indiscernible? Or is it just indiscernible with respect to the low-level properties postulated by a completed physics?

Many physicalists assume that if world w_1 and world w_2 do not differ in the low-level properties postulated by a completed physics, they will not differ in any of the higher-level physical properties either. The higher-level properties and the existence of the complex objects that have them both have to do with the way the basic particles and their properties fit together. That is, once you've got all the events happening at the most basic level (which we usually think of as the smallest in size and shortest in duration) and all the basic relations between the basic things, you have all of the rest. A nonbasic physical fact's obtaining simply amounts to a certain complex combination of basic physical facts' obtaining.

A theological metaphor borrowed from Kripke (1997) may be helpful here. By Thursday of the week of creation, God has decided exactly what all the molecules, or atoms, or quarks, or whatever the bottom level of stuff is, will be doing, where, and when. Does he have to come back Friday and decide if the Atlantic Ocean will be salty, or if there will be snow on Mount Everest? No, his work is done, as far as the physical part of the world goes.

Given that picture, there is no real difference between the requirements of the first paragraph and the requirements of the second. Why then the difference in formulation?

I think Chalmers wants the physicalist to focus on the question of where he can put the phenomenal properties. Will God's work up through Thursday determine when and where they occur? Or will he have to go back to work Friday and make those decisions? It seems that the phenomenal properties must be in one of the following categories:

A. Low-level properties postulated by a completed physics, which I'll call "basic physical properties."

B. Complex physical properties: properties that can be identified with conjunctions, disjunctions, or other first-order logical constructions from basic properties. (A) and (B) together I'll call "first-order physical properties."

C. Second-order physical properties: properties of the form "has a first-order physical property that meets condition C" where whether a property meets condition C depends only on first-order physical facts. These properties "logically supervene" on physical facts. (The use of "logic" is a little confusing; it is used here is a somewhat broader and looser sense than in (B). Logical supervenience is contrasted with causal supervenience; the latter calls for new facts, the former only for new ways of organizing and classifying them, ways that may go beyond the strict techniques implied by logic in (B). If one understands the principle of classification one can see that the supervening property is present in certain situations simply as a matter of meaning or logic, broadly conceived.)

If the phenomenal properties are in any of these categories, God is done Thursday evening. He doesn't have to come back to work Friday to decide which phenomenal properties to add and where to attach them. But he has more work to do if phenomenal properties belong in either of the following categories:

D. Properties that are not in (B) or (C) but causally supervene on (A).

E. Properties that neither logically nor causally supervene on (A).

Let's eliminate (E) as contrary to the overarching scientific hypotheses of our time (and at any rate not the position of either Chalmers or the antecedent physicalist). That leaves (A)–(D). (A)–(C) would leave subjective characters as clearly physical properties. (C) differs from (A) and (B), however, in that the subjective characters could not be *identified* with physical properties, neither the basic ones nor those definable from them by logical techniques. Still, if a brain state's having a subjective character simply amounts to its having certain basic physical properties, then even if for some reason the exact combination required can't be captured by logical techniques, we don't seem to have a property that is nonphysical in any respect that has much metaphysical bite. It might be, for example, that the property of being a valve belongs in class (C), but the existence of valves still wouldn't seem to be very interesting from a metaphysical point of view.[6]

If a property belongs to class (A), (B), or (C), then, there will not be two logically possible worlds, indiscernible in terms of basic physical properties and the laws that govern them, one of which has the property and the other of which does not. If it is case (C), a logically supervenient property, the occurrence of the supervenient property is not an extra fact; having the physical goings on amounts to having the supervenient property.

(D) requires something more than this. If a property is causally supervenient, there will be pairs of logically possible worlds, physically indiscernible at the level of basic physical properties and the laws that govern them, in one of which the property is exemplified and in the other of which it is not. By late Thursday afternoon, God will have narrowed down the world he is going to create to a set of worlds that are physically indistinguishable, alike in their (A), (B) and (C) properties, but different in their (D) properties. God will have to add a law or laws to nature, saying that in certain physical circumstances, these properties will occur. Given these laws, the occurrence of phenomenal properties will be causally determined by the occurrence of physical properties but will not simply amount to the their occurrence. It will be something more, something additional. (D) properties seem to be a version of what used to be called "emergent properties."

The target of the zombie argument, I think, is a philosopher for whom the live choices are (C) and (D). It might seem fair to ignore (A) and (B) for two reasons. First, it seems that twin arguments and multiple realizability arguments have convinced most philosophers that (A) and (B) are not viable; the most clearly physical status the physicalist can plausibly claim for mental states is some kind of supervenience. Second, since supervenience is a weaker form of physicalism than identity, if we can eliminate (C) as a possibility, we don't need to worry about (A) and (B).

Let's review the reasoning behind the move to supervenience. We'll start with a pretty plausible case, the property of being a valve.

Why do we suppose that a property like being a valve might be only logically supervenient on basic physical properties, rather than identifiable with them? It seems that we usually have one or both of two things in mind. First, the question of whether something is a valve (or a dollar, or a husband, or a sentence of English) might not depend just on the local physical properties of the thing but also on various contextual and historical facts: how it was created, where, and the like. Twin arguments bring home this point. One might have two identical structures, one of which was a valve and one of which was device for pitting prunes. The valve would be a valve in virtue of the reason for which it was made, who made it, where it was sold, and what it was used for, and the prune pitter would be a prune pitter for analogous reasons. You might be able to use the prune pitter for a valve; perhaps you could even turn the prune pitter into a valve. But the prune pitter pitting prunes is not a valve, even if its structure is identical to the valve in the next room controlling the flow of water into the prune scrubber.

Second, because it is the capacity to perform a certain function that makes a thing eligible to be a valve, things with indefinitely many physical configurations and compositions might serve. Multiple realizability examples make this point. Two structures that are quite different might both be valves, because they were manufactured, sold, bought, and used to control the flow of water.

We have then cases of "physical twins" that differ in certain properties that depend on historical and contextual factors. And we have dissimilar physical things that share properties because they can perform the same function. There are just lots of ways to be a valve. In such a case, it seems that a straightforward identification of the property of being a valve with a basic physical property or even a first-order physical property will likely not be possible.

It seems that many mental properties, the ones Chalmers calls "psychological properties," are like being a valve in both ways. Twin arguments point to the nonlocal, externalist nature of many such properties. (Recall the example involving Moravcsik and Flickinger in chapter 2.) Multiple realization cases point to the functional nature of many mental properties. In all of these cases, it seems that logical supervenience, level (C), is the appropriate relation between the physical world and the mental states. If we fix all of the physical facts, a physicalist will claim, we will fix these functional facts.

Martians are often appealed to in discussions of mental states and supervenience. Consider a standard philosophical Martian and me. His biology is based on different substances than mine. But the functions it serves are the same. We both can be in the *psychological* state of pain, even though our brain states are not the same. What we have in common is that the quite different states we are in share some (suitably abstract) causal role. We both have a barrier between us and the outside world: mine is skin, his is something else. We both have ways of exiting situations. We both have ways of getting help from others. And we both have an internal state that typically occurs when our barrier is stressed and typically leads to attempts to exit and/or get help. Our two quite different states share the causal role of pain. The psychological state of pain then logically supervenes on the first-order physical properties. So far so good.

Suppose now that we were convinced of two things. First, that the Martian and I, since we were functionally just alike, not only were both in the *psychological state of pain*, but were also in the same *phenomenal* state. What it was like for the Martian when he stepped on the tack that almost punctured his barrier to the outside world was just what it was like for me when I stepped on the tack that almost punctured my skin. Second, that, as was deemed common sense two chapters back, what it is like to be in pain depends on what goes on inside us at the moment of pain; that the what-it-is-like aspect of the state is not a causal, historical, or functional property.

If we adopt (C) with respect to subjective characters, we can get the first thing we want. We can say that not only the psychological state of pain but also the phenomenal state of pain logically supervenes on causal role and function. So the Martian and I are in the same phenomenal state. But this won't get us the second thing we want: that my experiences are a matter of what is going on inside of me, not a matter of how what is going on inside of me fits into the rest of the world.

The Martian and I are in different first-order states. We are in the same second-order causal/functional state, but that does not suffice to put us in the same phenomenal state, if that is a local, inner, first-order state. Something more is required. Using the theological metaphor, we require a decision by God to grace the Martian's Mars-brain states and my human brain states with the same subjective character. God has to decide that functionally equivalent states should cause the same subjective character. But that would amount to (D), causal supervenience. And of course if God could have made the decision to grace both the Martian and me with the same subjective characters, he could also have made the decision to take the day off and grace nobody with any qualia: the Chalmers zombie world. Subjective characters cannot be identified with functional states, the argument goes, and so must causally supervene upon them.

If I were convinced that (C) or (D) were correct, and I had to be either a functionalist about subjective characters, contrary to common sense, or a dualist, I would either go for (D) or take early retirement. But I don't see any argument for the restriction to (C) and (D). The reasonable way out of this dilemma between (C) and (D) is to ignore it and choose (B). Subjective characters are first-order physical states. We should reject supervenience and accept an identity theory for phenomenal states. We should reject both (C) and (D) and accept (B).

The antecedent physicalist rejects the argument that logical supervenience is a weaker relation than identity and so that if logical supervenience won't work, identity won't either. As we saw in chapter 1, the identity of a and b requires that a and b be one thing, sharing all properties. This is a heavy demand on a and b, and in this sense identity is stronger than logical supervenience. But identity does not put as heavy a demand on the terms "*a*" and "*b*" as logical supervenience does. With logical supervenience there are two ways of describing phenomena, one of which is derivative and logically explicable in terms of the other. Satisfying the more basic set of conditions will amount to satisfying the supervening conditions. Even if an exact definition cannot be given, we can explain why different physical systems, because they can function in certain ways, meet the conditions for being a valve. If the phenomenal concept of pain supervened on physical concepts, we should be able to give this sort of explanation of why various combinations of physical states count as or amount to or constitute pain states. That doesn't seem to make sense. That demand can't be met. So we have to give up on (C). We need to find some relation that does *not* make that problematic demand.

If (B) also made the demand, (D) would be the only place to go. But (B) doesn't make the problematic demand either, as I pointed out in chapter 1. Both causal supervenience and identity are *weaker* relations in this respect than logical supervenience. Neither requires the definition, analysis, or explication of a phenomenal concept of experience in terms of the way physical states function. The physicalist need not retreat to causal supervenience but should stick instead with identity.

This means that we will have to accept that the Martian and I are not in the same phenomenal state. But what reason is there to suppose that we are? It seems to me that whatever reason we thought we had was based on ignoring the Block-Chalmers distinction between psychological states and phenomenal states. Can we accept this consequence?

To suppose that the Martian and I are not in the same phenomenal states, it is not necessary to deny that Martians have any phenomenal states at all. Some of the internal states of Martians may be like something to be in. We may find that our psychology fits the Martian very well. We may find we can predict and control our Martian using the same basic framework of desires, intentions, emotions, beliefs, goals, fears, and the like as we use for ourselves. If so, there will be a place in his psychology for pain and pleasure, for our psychology could not begin to fit onto a being that was not motivated by pleasures and pains.

One often compares Martians and robots in discussions of supervenience as two sorts of alien beings with respect to which the denial or affirmation of consciousness might be an issue. But there are big differences. Martians would presumably be naturally occurring beings evolved on Mars. If we find our belief and desire psychology fits them, we have reason to suppose that the basic architecture of their mentality is like ours, that their intentionality is, as Searle says, "natural" and not manufactured. With any robots that now exist or are likely to, the case will be quite different. Their susceptibility to intentional description will have been planned by their creators. I do not mean to say that robots could not have natural intentionality and could not have what seems to me a requirement of it: phenomenal pains and pleasures that their basic architecture motivates them to avoid and seek. But I see no reason to suppose that the robots now envisaged do so.

4.4   The Inverted Spectrum

After his exposition of the zombie argument, Chalmers notes that such a dramatic possibility as a zombie world is not required for the dualist argument:

It suffices to establish the logical possibility of a world physically identical to ours in which the facts about conscious experience are merely *different* from the facts in our world, without conscious experience being absent entirely. As long as some positive fact about experience in our world does not hold in a physically identical world, then consciousness does not logically supervene. . . .

It is therefore enough to note that one can coherently imagine a physically identical world in which conscious experiences are *inverted*, or (at the local level) imagine a being physically identical to me but with inverted conscious experiences. One might imagine, for example, that where I have a red experience, my inverted twin has a blue experience, and vice versa. Of course he will call his blue experiences "red," but that is irrelevant. What matters is that the experience he has of the things we both call "red"—blood, fire engines, and so on—is of the same kind as the experience I have of the things we both call "blue," such as the sea and sky. . . .

[A]s a *logical* possibility, it seems entirely coherent that experiences could be inverted while physical structure is duplicated exactly. Nothing in the neurophysiology dictates that one sort of processing should be accompanied by red experiences rather than by yellow experiences. (Chalmers 1996, 99–100)

The possibility of inverted spectra has been thought about for a long time and used in different ways in the philosophy of language and mind. When it is used for different purposes, the details are not always the same. The key question is: what has to stay constant while the subjective characters shift? When I was a graduate student in the 1960s the use of language and other observable behaviors were held constant. Some of my teachers drew the conclusion that since changes in experience wouldn't show up in behavior, there was something fishy about experience; others drew the conclusion that the various forms of logical behaviorism were wrong.[7]

The latter use of the argument is legitimate and convincing. If behavior, including language use, is all that we hold constant across the individuals with different color experiences, it is clear that inverted spectrum cases are possible and to some extent no doubt actually occur. That there are individual differences in the color experiences sighted people have is clear from various forms of color-blindness, and the fact that color-blindness is hard to discover shows how easy it is for differences in color experience to be hard to detect at the level of language and behavior. That there are other individual differences, and that there might be a case in which things were perfectly shifted in some way, seems to me quite possible (see Nida-Rümelin 1997). I am inclined to agree with Block that we "simply do not know if spectrum inversion obtains or not" (Block 1990). (Shoemaker provides some reasons for thinking it does not in Shoemaker 1997.)

It does not follow from the success of these versions of the inverted spectrum argument that a version of the inverted spectrum argument will be useful to Chalmers, for it does not follow that what Chalmers claims to be possible is possible. For Chalmers' purposes, not only must the physical facts involved with language and observable behavior be held constant, and not only the functions of the color sensations, but *all* the physical facts that are in any way relevant to color experiences, down to the finest details of chemical processes in the rods and cones—the place where the differences in color experiences that we know of have their origin—and beyond, including events in the visual cortex and anywhere else relevant to vision and the experience of it. The plausibility of the inverted spectrum case in the context of an argument against logical behaviorism simply does not carry over to a case against antecedent physicalism. Thus, as with the zombie case, we can grant Chalmers the first requirement of his alternative possible world: we have twins with color experiences systematically inverted relative to our own, and these inversions do not lead to any differences in linguistic or other behavior. But there is no reason to grant him the second requirement: that some of these worlds are physically indiscernible from our own. If the antecedent physicalist is right, none will be.

We will return briefly to the zombie and inverted spectrum arguments in chapter 8, when we consider the purest form of the modal argument. There we will consider the framework of primary and secondary possibilities that Chalmers uses to present his argument. By that point we will be in a position to see how a certain resistance to the considerations presented in this chapter is built into that machinery and his use of it.

a red thing. She learns an additional fact about that experience, a fact that involves this what-it-is-like property. It then wasn't one of the physical facts, and physicalism is false.

In this chapter I'll first spend some time locating the item of knowledge that is supposed to lead to the problem. I'll introduce some other cases that will help us focus on just what is problematic about this bit of knowledge. I'll argue that this bit of knowledge is of a species I call *recognitional* knowledge. Then I'll argue that for any philosopher, dualist, or physicalist, who accepts a certain view of knowledge that I call the "subject matter assumption," recognitional knowledge poses a problem. In the next chapter, I'll try to provide an account of recognitional knowledge that will enable us to understand what Mary learns.

5.2   Locating the Problem

Mary leaves the room. She looks at a ripe tomato. She knows ripe tomatoes are red. She has the experience of seeing a red object for the first time. She learns something. What is it she learns?

Here are some candidates for how she might express her knowledge:

(1)   This is what it is like to have my present experience.

(2)   This is what it is like for me now to see red.

(3)   This is what it is like to see red.

(3) is to be taken in the sense of "this is what it is like for me to see red now, and what it would have been like for me to see red before, and what it is and has been and will be like for others to see red, in normal conditions with normal eyesight."

First consider (1). It seems clear that this is something Mary didn't know ahead of time. And (1) expresses something that she learns. It seems that it is a contingent fact that her experience is the way it in fact is and that Mary knows what it is like. So there is some knowledge here. (1) doesn't actually communicate what she learns, for the person who hears (1) is not having Mary's experience and so doesn't know exactly to which subjective character she is attending.

(1) refers to a certain occurrence that Mary didn't know about before, since it didn't exist before. For this reason, Jackson says this knowledge is not the problem for the physicalist:

> [T]he knowledge Mary lacked which is of particular point for the knowledge argument against physicalism is knowledge about the experiences of others, not about her own. When she is let out, she has new experiences, color experiences she has never had before. It is not, therefore, an objection to physicalism that she learns something on being let out. Before she was let out, she could not have known facts about her experiences of red for there were no such facts to know. That physicalist and nonphysicalist alike can agree on. After she is let out, things change; and physicalism can happily admit that she learns this; after all, some physical things will change, for instance her brain states and their functional roles. (Jackson 1997, 393)

So it seems that the antecedent physicalist need not worry about the new knowledge that Mary expresses with (1).

Given this, it seems that (2) is not a problem either. Mary knew while in her room that ripe tomatoes were red and what they looked like. There is no reason for her not to have known those things. So she recognizes what she is looking at as a ripe tomato and infers that it is red and that she is seeing red. This knowledge, together with the unproblematic (1), allows her to infer (2).

It must be (3), then, that gives the physicalist the problem, because (3) seems to be the sort of thing Mary should have known in the Jackson room, if she knew everything. (3) expresses a fact about the nature of a certain kind of experience people have. The "this" refers to a type of experience, a subjective character that can be the character of many experiences of many people. (3) says that the normal experience of seeing red is of that type, has that character. Mary is using her new experience as an exemplar of the type in order to refer to the type. Though not itself a problem, (1) plays an important role. The subjective character Mary attends to in (1) is the one she takes to be characteristic of normal red-seeing in (3). (3) was true before Mary had her experience. So if (3) is a physical fact, it could have been and should have been included in the texts Mary read in the black and white room, and she should already know it. Normal red-seeing was something she was supposed to know all about in the black and white room. But she doesn't already know it. So it wasn't included in what she read. So it isn't a physical fact. That's the problem.

As the quote above continues, Jackson makes this point but also says some things that do not follow from what he told us about Mary's situation:

The trouble for physicalism is that, after Mary sees her first ripe tomato, she will realize how impoverished her conception of the mental life of *others* has been *all along*. She will realize that there was, all the time she was carrying out her laborious investigations into the neurophysiologies of others and into the functional roles of their internal states, something about these people she was quite unaware of. All along their experiences . . . had a feature conspicuous to them but until now hidden from her (in fact, not in logic). But she knew all the physical facts about them all along; hence, what she did not know until her release is not a physical fact about their

experiences. But it is a fact about them. That is the trouble for physicalism. (Jackson 1997, 393)

I don't see why Jackson says some of these things. As I
imagine Mary, she is in the Jackson room, reading, perhaps
writing, books about the physics and biology of color vision. She knows that people have experiences when they see
things (as she does) and that these experiences have subjective characters (as hers do). She is aware that she is in a black
and white room and so isn't having color experiences. But I
don't see why she shouldn't know that others have them.

This ignorance of the fact that other people have color experiences (as opposed to simply failing to know what it's
like to have them) was not part of the original setup and is
not necessary to feel the problem of Mary's new knowledge,
so I think perhaps it is simply hyperbole. If subjective characters are physical aspects of experiences, as the antecedent
physicalist maintains, then if Mary knows all of the physical facts, she will know about subjective characters. For the
dualist to assume that she knows all of the physical facts
without knowing of the occurrence of subjective characters
is for the dualist to beg the question against the antecedent
physicalist.

The antecedent physicalist, on the other hand, is not begging the question here. Our inquiry is whether, given that
one is antecedently inclined toward physicalism, Mary's experiences and arguments based on them give one any reason to give it up. The antecedent physicalist may suppose
that there have been investigations to identify the physical
aspects of experiences that correlate with judgments of similarity in what it's like to have those experiences. Subjective
characters can be labeled in terms of their physical causes,
and much may have been learned about them.

Let us suppose then that Mary's texts have systematically named the subjective characters of color experiences. Q_R is defined in one of Mary's texts as the subjective character that people with normal vision see when they look at a red object, such as a fire hydrant or a ripe tomato, in ordinary daylight. The text does not take a position on whether Q_R is a physical aspect of the brain or some other kind of property. So Mary knows that Q_R is involved in seeing red in normal circumstances. She knows that it is also an aspect of some illusory or deceptive experiences that are not cases of seeing red things. She may know of a lot of experiments that have been conducted to isolate Q_R. And if we are not epiphenomenalists, we may suppose that her physical knowledge includes facts about what experiences with different subjective characters bring about. None of this means that she knows what it's like to have experiences with these subjective characters or denies that she would learn this when she leaves the room, so it is not begging the question or ignoring the problem.

So let's assume that Mary does have a concept of Q_R that is actually quite rich. It contains a number of things that mine does, such as being the subjective character of normal red experiences, but a great deal more that she has gleaned from her textbooks. It doesn't, however, contain any Humean ideas of color impressions, any memory images. Her own experiences have not been a direct source of information for these concepts of color sensations, and the concepts have never been applied to color sensations of her own.

I think Jackson must really be supposing that Mary is in more or less this situation, for otherwise it is difficult to see how she learns about the experiences of others when she has color experiences herself. I assume that he has something like this in mind. Mary sees a ripe tomato. She knows that

ripe tomatoes are red. She knows her color vision is normal.[9]
So she knows that the experience she is having is seeing red
and reasons that what it is like for her to have the experience is more or less what it is like for others to have the
experience of seeing red. But this requires the background
assumption that there is something it is like to see red; that
the people outside the Jackson room have color qualia and
so have something she has heretofore lacked. If Mary didn't
know this, it is unclear why her reaction to her new experience wouldn't be, "Gosh, I wonder if other people have this
sort of thing happen." She would have no good reason to
advance from (1) to (3).

What is puzzling about Mary for the antecedent physicalist is best seen as an instance of the sort of problem Frege
called to our attention: how can identities be informative
(Frege 1892)? Starting with where we left off, we have Mary
realizing

(3)   This is what it is like to see red.

In the black and white room, based on her extensive study
of the literature, Mary learned (4):

(4)   Subjective character Q_R is the subjective character of
seeing red.

and so she can now infer (5), the version of Mary's new
knowledge that we'll take as our official Frege problem:

(5) Q_R is this subjective character.

Mary had a belief she might have expressed with (4) before leaving the black and white room, as we are imagining
things. It simply acknowledges the definition of Q_R from
her text. After she began to have color experiences and her

experiences were connected with various objects whose colors were known to her, she held a belief she could have expressed with (3) during a period in which she was experiencing red. Combining these, she ends up with (5). If we ask now what the difference is between what she knew and expressed with (4) and what she knows and expresses with (5), it seems to me that we have a fair statement of the problem Mary poses for the antecedent physicalist.

Clearly (5) differs from (4): Mary knew the one, but not the other, while in the Jackson room. If (5) constitutes new knowledge, it must contain new content. The truth-conditions of (4) and (5) must differ in some way.

Max Black no doubt had Frege's problem in mind when he objected to J. J. C. Smart that even if we identify experiences with brain states, there is still the question of what makes the brain state an experience and the experience it is; it seems that must be an additional property the brain state has (Smart 1959). There must be a property that serves as our mode of presentation of the experience as an experience. Black would no doubt have enjoyed the knowledge argument. He might say, "But then isn't there something about Q_R that Mary didn't learn in the Jackson room that explains the difference between 'Q_R is Q_R,' which she already knew in the Jackson room, and (5), which she didn't? There must a new mode of presentation of that state to which Q_R refers, which is to say some additional *and apparently nonphysical* aspect of that state that she learned about only when she exited the room that explains why (5) is *new* knowledge?"[10]

5.3 Raising Suspicions

It is not easy to say what Mary's new knowledge is. I try to do so in the next two chapters. The point I want to make

Table 5.1
Two More Separate Issues

	Accept Subject Matter Assumption	Reject Subject Matter Assumption
Physicalism	A problem with Mary	No problem with Mary
Dualism	A problem with Mary	No problem with Mary

in the remainder of this chapter is that there is no reason to think that the difficulties involved are special problems for *physicalism*. The culprit, I believe, is a certain doctrine about knowledge, one that crept into the problem with the remark in setting up the problem. As I put it: "Mary learns everything there is to know about the physical world, for after all, what is known can be written down and she can read it." This remark relies on what I call the "subject matter assumption." I won't fully explain the connection between the remark and the assumption until the next chapter, however. The plan of attack is analogous to that of the last chapter. I'll claim that just as epiphenomenalism is the real issue with the zombie argument, the subject matter assumption is the real issue with the knowledge argument. The situation, I will claim, is that represented in table 5.1.

Before saying what the subject matter assumption is, I am going to tell one joke, describe two more thought experiments involving people kept in rooms in which arguments similar to the knowledge argument can be deployed, and look at a variation on Mary's case, due to Martine Nida-Rümelin. The point of all this is to arouse the reader's suspicions about the knowledge argument and get her grey cells moving in the right direction for the next chapter.

Larry, Lost in Time

The first case is simply a reworking of part of McTaggart's famous argument against the reality of time (McTaggart 1921,
1927). What McTaggart calls the B-series is all of the facts
about what events happen in what order: which events are
before which, and which are simultaneous. Metaphysically,
it seems that all events fall into the B-series somewhere. So a
representation of the B-series ought to contain all the information there is concerning which events occur before, after,
and at the same time as others. More realistically, a representation of all the events of a certain kind during a certain
time period ought to contain all the information one needs
about events of that kind during that period. Imagine a *TV
Guide,* or an appointment book that's all filled in for a certain date. These seem to provide all of the information one
could need about the evening's television programs or the
next day's appointments. But the appointment book and the
TV Guide won't do you much good unless you know what
day it is when you are consulting them, and that information
is hard to print in a *TV Guide* or to enter into an appointment
book. Without some *annotation* of the day, the *TV Guide* and
the appointment book leave you in a position a bit like the
one in which Terry finds himself in the old joke:

Terry: You know I've really enjoyed talking to you. I'd like
to see you again. Can I have your number?

Fran: It's in the book.

Terry: And what's your name?

Fran: It's in the book too.

The phone book may contain all the numbers, including
Fran's, but it won't do Terry much good. Terry wants the

phone number of *that person,* and that's a hard piece of information for the phone company to print in the book. You need your appointments for *today,* and the television shows for *this evening.* Where in the B-series do we find, or put, the information that we express with "Today is April 1, 1999"? The problem can be put into the form of a knowledge argument:

Suppose that it is April 1, 1999, and we are all in a room at the Claremont Hotel in Berkeley, California, where a symposium on the philosophy of Hugh Mellor is being held at the Pacific Division Meetings of the American Philosophical Association. Across the hall, unknown to us, there is a young man named Larry, who was raised in a room in the Claremont Hotel with no annotated calendars. That is, he is never allowed to know what day it is or even what year it is. This young man has a passionate interest in the Pacific Division of the APA, and is allowed to read all of the APA publications there ever have been, including programs of all of the past APAs and also future APAs for the next twenty years. (Let's pretend that Anita Silvers, executive director of the Pacific Division, is part of this experiment, and that, motivated in part by a terrific deal on printing programs that is available only for a limited amount of time, she has decided on the schedule of talks for the next twenty years. She will rely on her vast knowledge of the membership of the Pacific APA to make sure things turn out right, making deft suggestions to the key committee members at the right times.) So Larry knows all the B-facts there are to know about events at the APA meetings: which talks come before which talks, which sessions are concurrent, and so forth. He knows, for example, that in 1999 on April 1 there was or will be a meeting about the views of Hugh Mellor. He knows also:

(6)   The 1999 Presidential Address is on April 2, 1999.

Every odd-numbered year he can tell when the Pacific APA meetings are starting because he can see, from the small window in his room, the sign out in front of the Claremont that says, "Welcome Pacific Division, APA."[11] But he doesn't know what year it is. Larry waits patiently for his release, for he is proud to be part of a philosophical experiment.

Larry has just been released, stepped out of the room in which he was kept, and joined us here at the symposium. Larry peeks at the Palm Pilot of the person sitting next to him, sees the first up-to-date calendar he has ever seen, and realizes:

(7)   Today is April 1, 1999.

and from that and what he already knew already, he infers

(8)   The 1999 Pacific Division APA Presidential Address is tomorrow.

Clearly (8) is *new knowledge* for Larry. (8) expresses something that Larry did not know before his release, whereas (6) expresses something he did know before his release. So (6) and (8) seem to be different bits of knowledge. And they both seem to be APA-facts in the sense above, facts about when the APA sessions are held. But (8) cannot be identified with (6), since Larry knew (6) without knowing (8). The same goes for any other of the APA-facts Larry knew. Did Anita Silvers leave something out of those programs?

There are two levels on which we can think about what happened to Larry, which I'll call "the information flow level" and "the content level." The first has to do with how information flows between Larry's various ideas. At the last moment he is trapped in the room, Larry has two ideas that are *of* the day April 1, 1999. One is the idea he associates with a certain page in his calendar, labeled "April 1, 1999," on which he has scrupulously entered all the APA events scheduled for that date. The other is the idea he would express with the word "today." This idea is tied to his present perceptions of what is going on around him. We can imagine that corresponding to this idea he has kept a journal, each page devoted to a day, but with no dates, on which he records observations about each day as it passes, with the page on top serving as the repository for information about the present day. Today that page is numbered 2987.

The two notions are connected to April 1, 1999, in quite different ways. The first notion, which gets information from and adds information to his calendar, is associated with that day because of the date printed in the calendar. He writes things on that page that he sees connected with that date in the APA programs. The page in his journal is connected to that day because that is the page he uses on that day to record his perceptions: "not a cloud in the sky," and "lots of noise in the halls," and so forth.

The two notions are also connected with different information sources. The first is associated with information about APA events, whose source was the programs left in his room. The second is associated with current perceivable events, mostly weather and noise.

From the point of view of the flow of information, what happens seems relatively easy to say. The two notions become *linked* when he sees today's date on the Palm Pilot and information flows between them. He now paper-clips today's page from his journal to the April 1 page in his calendar, and something along the same lines happens in his mind. All the ideas that were associated with either notion are now associated with one.

If Larry has new knowledge, however, mustn't the *content* of his knowledge have changed in some way?

But has it? We usually take the *content* of a belief to be the conditions that the *subject matter* of the belief has to meet for the belief to be true. By subject matter, I mean the people, things, places, times, properties, and relations that the notions and ideas involved in the belief are *of*. Larry's own *ideas* are not the subject matter of his belief; rather, the days he thinks about, and the events that happen on them, and the speakers and rooms in the Claremont are their subject matter. But then we have a problem, for *Larry's beliefs impose exactly the same conditions on their subject matter after the event of recognition as before.*

Consider Larry's calendar and journal. Take the combination of them, before pages are paper-clipped to one another. For the calendar to be true, the Mellor symposium must happen on April 1, 1999. For the journal to be true, April 1, 1999, must be a cloudless day in Berkeley. If both are true, the Mellor symposium must be held on a cloudless day. The paper-clipping of the one page to the other makes no difference in the requirements the truth of his system of calendar and journal put on April 1, 1999. And the same is true of the linking of ideas in his system of beliefs.[12]

Yet it is easy to see what additional truth-condition is added when the April 1 page of the calendar and the latest page of the journal are clipped together with the intention of merging the records. If the pages are not of the same day, the records will be false. And when Larry's notion of April 1 is linked to his notion of "today," the notion that gets the information from his present perceptions about what the day is like, his system of beliefs can be true only if those two notions are connected, in their different ways, to the same day.

Of course, if you think about it, that requirement was already there, too. *Given* that (say) page 91 in the calendar is assigned to April 1, 1999, by the date printed on it, and *given* that page 2987 of Larry's journal is assigned to April 1, 1999, by the fact that it is used to record the events of that day, they must co-refer. What changes when Larry clips the two pages is that it is now required for the truth of the system of journal and calendar that they co-refer *independently of those givens*. The point is clearer if Larry makes a mistake, in his excitement, and links page 2986 of his journal to the April 1 page of his calendar. Each page is wholly true before the link is made (or so we may assume). But once the link is made, falsity arises.

Let's return to the case in which Larry gets things right. The linking then makes not only an information flow difference, but a semantic difference, a difference in the truth-conditions of the system of ideas or notebooks. But this semantic difference, this difference in truth-conditions, has to do with the representations, the ideas or notebook pages, not with the subject matter. It seems puzzling to appeal to it, for it seems that Larry's new knowledge is not about his ideas or his notebook pages.

Gary, Lost in Wyoming

Gary is in an even less inviting situation than Larry and also one that is less likely to provoke philosophical theories. Gary has been trapped for a month in a windowless hut across from Little America, just off Interstate 80 in western Wyoming. (Little America is a gas station with a restaurant and souvenir shop. It has more gas pumps than any place in the world.) He has memorized an interstate road map. Larry knows all the facts about the locations of things along Interstate 80: the order of states, cities, towns, and villages as one progresses west to east along Interstate 80, from Berkeley through Reno, Salt Lake City, Little America, Cheyenne, Lincoln, and on through the mysterious East. But he isn't allowed to look out of his hut, so he doesn't know where he is. Eventually he escapes. He sees all the gas pumps, realizes he is in Little America, and immediately knows a number of facts that seem to be facts about where things are along Interstate 80 but that he didn't know before. He already knew:

(9)   Salt Lake City is southwest of Little America.

Now he learns:

(10)   This place is Little America.

and infers

(11)   Salt Lake City is southwest of this place.

And so on for many other things. What is the difference between (9) and (11)? Was something left out of Gary's interstate road map?

Here again, it seems easy enough to say what happens at the level of information flow. Gary has an notion *of* Little America tied to his present perception. Associated with this notion are such ideas as "being across the interstate from me." He has another notion of Little America, one he has had for years, crammed full of ideas gleaned from experiences he had there before being captured and from his wide reading. In particular he knows that it is called "Little America," that there is a warm and friendly gift shop and restaurant there, where hungry and thirsty strangers are always welcome, and that it is north and east of Salt Lake City. When the similarities between the ideas associated with his perception and the ones associated with his old notion pile up, recognition happens. Information flows between the ideas. He realizes that the place across the street has a warm gift shop where he will be welcome and realizes that Salt Lake City is to the west and south.

Again, the subject matter content of Gary's beliefs, before recognition occurred, required that the place across the highway be northeast of Salt Lake City and have a warm and friendly gift shop. The two different notions are both of the same place, Little America. So for the beliefs associated with each notion to be true, the place they are both about has to have all of the properties associated with either. The link that allows information to flow between the two, that motivates Gary's hike across the street and his inference that Salt Lake City is to the south and west, seems to have no effect whatsoever on this content.

To see its effect, we need to abstract from one or more of the connections. Again it is helpful to imagine a mistake. Suppose Gary is actually looking at Elwood's Oasis, a place a hundred or so miles down the interstate from Little America. Once he makes the link, a new requirement is imposed on his system of beliefs, one that makes them false. Once the link is made, the system can be true only if the perception and the notion are of the same place. When a mistake is made, this link provokes a number of changes in the conditions imposed by the truth of the beliefs on the subject matter; for example, Elwood's Oasis would have to have a gift shop, which it doesn't.

This basic semantic difference is the same when a mistake is not made, but then no new subject matter conditions are imposed. In the case in which Gary is looking at Little America, the same requirement is added: that the perception and the notion are of the same place. In this case, no new conditions are imposed on the subject matter. The old ones are imposed in a new way. This new requirement on Gary's own notions and perceptions seems to be where we need to look for his new knowledge. And yet it seems odd that Gary's new knowledge should be about his own perceptions and notions rather than about Little America.

What about Mary?

Let's now change the Mary story just slightly. When Mary gets out of the Jackson room, she is led into a sort of plaid room, which I'll call the Nida-Rümelin room.[13] The wallpaper exhibits many patches of different colors, but there is no hint for Mary as to which is which. At this point she will have the experiences she hasn't had before, of red and yellow and blue and so forth. But she won't know of which colors they are experiences.

During her time in the Nida-Rümelin room, Mary may notice many things about the colors she sees. She may notice that the red patches and pink patches are much more like one another than either is like the blue patches. She may decide she likes the experience of looking at green best of all. Of course, her thinking won't involve these names for the colors, although she may introduce some herself. Let's suppose she calls red "wow." And given her scientific background, she introduces into her own thinking the systematic term Q_{wow} for the subjective character of the experience of seeing wow.

Mary now has two concepts of red and two concepts of the subjective character of the experience of seeing red. One of the latter she has had for a while, since she first read about colors and their subjective characters while in the Jackson room. Among the ideas that are associated with this concept are the following: being called Q_R, being the subjective character that occurs when one sees red, being the topic of various papers and experiments, and whatever else was known about Q_R at the time the books Mary read were written. There are no memory images associated with this concept, and she is not applying it to her current experience of the red patch. Her other concept is new, formed when she saw the red patches in the plaid room. Among the ideas that are associated with it are: being called Q_{wow}, being the subjective character of the experience of seeing wow, being *this* subjective character (as she looks at a red patch), and memory images that allow her to recognize wow and Q_{wow} after a period of looking elsewhere in the room. The two concepts are of the same thing, Q_R, but this identity is not reflected in Mary's cognitive states; the concepts are not linked; information does not flow between them; that is, because she is allowed only in the Nida-Rümelin room where there are no tomatoes or fire hydrants, Mary does not *recognize* Q_R, the subjective character of red experiences, when she first encounters it. She will recognize it, however, when she is finally let out into the normal world and sees fire plugs, tomatoes, blood, and the like.

We cannot find Mary's new knowledge at the level of subject matter content, just as we could not with Larry and Gary. Mary *already* believed that Q_R was the subjective character of the experience of seeing red. Her new concept of Q_{wow} is also *of* Q_R. Before she leaves the Nida-Rümelin room, as she looks at the red patch, attends to her experience, and thinks, "This is Q_{wow}," Mary's thought can only be true if she is in state Q_R. She believes she is in state Q_{wow}, and in fact Q_{wow} is Q_R. When she leaves the Nida-Rümelin room, sees the tomato, realizes that Q_{wow} is Q_R and links the concepts, her beliefs will change. But the demands that the truth of her beliefs place on the world do not.

Mary has learned something, but what? The problem does not have anything special to do with dualism or physicalism. It is the same problem we have in the case of Gary and Larry, and, for that matter, Terry. It is, in fact, one species of Frege's problem. At the heart of each case is an informative identity either known or not known. It is natural to suppose that the key is the two different ways of thinking of the object, location, property, or state involved. But we cannot get this key to work the lock until we remove the subject matter assumption.

The knowledge argument looks at Mary and says to the physicalist, in effect: "You can't find the knowledge, because you can't find the fact, because you don't have enough subject matter. In addition to the physical properties, you need some nonphysical ones." However, this is no more true in Mary's case than in Gary's or Larry's. There is plenty that is puzzling, but it's not physicalism that is at the bottom of the puzzles. At the bottom is the subject matter assumption. The antecedent physicalist replies, "In Mary's case, as in Gary's, Larry's and Terry's, the need is not for nonphysical properties, but for a broader conception of the content of thought."

5.4   The Subject Matter Assumption

The subject matter assumption may be put succinctly and almost, it seems, tautologically, as follows:

The content of a belief is simply whatever is believed about whatever the belief is about.

Or, at greater length, as follows:

The rational content of a belief is that part of the full truth-conditions of the belief that accounts for the role the belief has in theoretical and practical inferences. The rational content of a belief is the conditions its truth puts on the subject matter of the belief, the objects the notions and concepts in the belief are of.

For a simple example suppose Elwood believes that Bill Clinton smokes cigars. We may suppose that the existence of this belief, given of course the whole rest of Elwood's cognitive system and the way it is embedded in the world, consists in the fact that his concept of smoking cigars is associated with his notion of Clinton. (And of course this way of speaking is just a way of saying that in whatever way our brains keeps track of data of this sort, the requisite change has occurred in Elwood's.) Call Elwood's notion of Clinton n_c and his concept of being a smoker I_S. For Elwood's belief to be true, the following proposition Q must be true:

Q: There is an object that is the object n_c is of, and it is a member of the set of objects that have the property that I_S is of.

It would be very odd to say that Elwood believes Q, or that Q is part of what Elwood believes, or anything like that. Elwood's belief is about Clinton and smoking cigars; that's the subject mater. What he believes is that Clinton does smoke cigars. Not being a philosopher but a resort owner, Elwood spends no time thinking about his ideas and notions, and the thought that Q would never occur to him.[14]

So Q is an example of what is at issue. Q is part of what needs to be the case for Elwood's belief to be true, but it is not part of what Elwood believes. Q is not about the subject matter of Elwood's belief, but about the components of the belief; it doesn't tell us how Clinton needs to be in order for the belief to be true, but how the belief *itself* and its components need to be related to the world for the belief to be true. For this reason, I call Q part of the *reflexive truth-conditions* of Elwood's belief, or part of the *reflexive content*. I think we need to reject the subject matter assumption, because the rational content of a belief includes its reflexive contents. The cases of Mary, Larry, Gary, and Terry should have provided some shape and plausibility to this idea. In the next chapter, I'll try to develop a positive account that explains why this is so.

6   Recognition and Identification

Suppose that all of mankind had been completely blind up to a certain point in history, and then acquired vision. . . . [We would] in principle be able to predict the relevant neural and behavioral processes, and thus to foretell all the discriminatory and linguistic behavior which depends upon the new cortical processes (which correspond to the emergent, novel qualities of experience). What is it then that we would not or could not know at the time of the original prediction? I think the answer is obvious. We would not and could not know (then) the color experiences by acquaintance; *i.e., (1) we would not* have them; *(2) we could not* imagine them; *(3) we could not* recognize (or label) *them as "red," "green," etc.*

—Herbert Feigl, *The "Mental" and the "Physical": The Essay and a Postscript*

So far I have given some reasons for suspecting that the knowledge argument may depend on an assumption that the physicalist need not and should not accept. In this chapter I begin to put forward a positive account of what is believed or known when the crucial identities such as

This$_i$ subjective character is Q_R

are accepted. This account will explain the origin of and limits of the subject matter assumption.

The details I seek to provide won't be physiological or neurological, nor even, for the most part, very phenomenological. They will be logical, semantical, and philosophical. I have argued that it is consistent with physicalism that there be a special way of accessing the what-it-is-like properties of our own brain states, available only to the person who is in the states. Recognizing that a given state known in another way, as the state of seeing red or the state Q_R, say, is the very state one is accessing in this special way does constitute new knowledge, and this is what happens in Mary's case. I have said that there is no problem here for physicalism. The problem is for an epistemology based on the subject matter assumption, an assumption that physicalism need not and should not embrace.

But there will be nagging doubts whether physicalism can really accommodate this new knowledge of Mary's. Black's old problem seems to rear its head at every turn (Smart 1959). Different modes of presentation and different pieces of knowledge, mean that somewhere, somehow, there is new content. The conditions for the truth of "Q_R is the sensation of red" are *not* the same as those of "Q_R is *this* subjective character." New content means a new property that Q_R is required to have by the second statement. Surely what Mary learns is that Q_R has this new property. But isn't that just the point of the knowledge argument? If this new property is a physical property, it seems it could be absorbed into the physical description of Q_R that Mary learned while in the Jackson room. But then it cannot be that property that constitutes her *new* knowledge about Q_R. It is this philosophical part of the problem on which I focus.

6.1 A Case of Recognition

Suppose that I have never met Fred Dretske, but I know who he is. As a matter of fact, suppose that I know every fact there is to know about which books Dretske has authored. Call these the Dretske-book facts, or the dretskical facts, for short. He has written, so far, *Seeing and Knowing*, *Knowledge and the Flow of Information*, *Explaining Behavior*, and *Naturalizing the Mind*. So I know, in particular,

(1)   Dretske wrote *Knowledge and the Flow of Information*.

I admire this book very much and have long wanted to meet and shake hands with its author.

Then one day I am at a party and I am standing next to someone. We chat for a while. He says some interesting things about knowledge and information, and so I begin explaining—not quite accurately, one might suppose—Dretske's ideas on the subject and recommend that my interlocutor go out and read *Knowledge and the Flow of Information*. "Well actually," he says, "I wrote *Knowledge and the Flow of Information*." At this point I learn something I could express with

(2)   You wrote *Knowledge and the Flow of Information*,

or, pointing to Dretske,

(3)   That man wrote *Knowledge and the Flow of Information*.

How did the content of my beliefs change when I acquired this knowledge?

In the beginning of the story, my beliefs about Dretske were *detached* from my current perception of him. After Dretske told me who he was, they became *attached*. Here is what

I mean by this. At the beginning of the story, I had beliefs about Dretske. These beliefs involved a notion of Dretkse associated with various ideas I had gotten from reading things by him and about him. The notion is sort of like internal file folder, and the ideas like information that has been put in such a folder. This inner file was set up when I first heard about and read articles by Dretske. This notion was not, at the beginning of the story, attached to any perception I was having.

When a notion is attached to a perception, the information one picks up perceptually modifies the ideas associated with the notion. If things go right, of course, the perception will be of the person or thing the notion is of. But the relation of attachment is independent of the relation of co-reference. Things can go quite wrong. Suppose for example that I have a perception of David Israel attached to my notion of Paul Newman. This is what happens when I see Israel and mistakenly take him to be Newman. My perception and my notion do not co-refer, but they are attached—by mistake. As a result I may tell people later, "Paul Newman is in Palo Alto."

At the beginning of the party, my mistake is the opposite of this one. My notion of Fred Dretske, the one I am drawing on to describe his views, and my perception of my interlocutor are in fact of the same individual, but they are not attached. I am perceiving a thin, average-sized man with an intense, slightly puzzled, slightly amused, slightly annoyed expression. I don't add these ideas to my Dretske notion. I don't have the belief that Dretske is puzzled, annoyed, amused, and talking to me.

Here is a picture of the way our beliefs are organized that will help make this clear. Think of the architecture of our beliefs as a three-story building. At the top level are detached files (ideas associated with notions), such as my beliefs about Dretske. At the bottom level are perceptions and perceptual buffers. Buffers are new notions associated with the perceptions and used to temporarily store ideas we gain from the perceptions until we can identify the individual, or form a permanent detached notion for him, or forget about him.

The middle level is full of informational wiring. Sockets dangle down from above, and plugs stick up from below. The ideas in the first-floor perceptual buffers and in the third-floor files are constantly compared. When there is a high probability that they are of a single person or thing, recognition (or misrecognition) occurs. The plug from the buffer is plugged into the socket for the notion. Information then flows both ways.

The information flowing up from the perception adds new ideas to the file associated with the notion. So in the Israel-Newman case, the idea of being in Palo Alto is added to my Newman file. The information flowing down to the bottom level enriches the perceptual buffer and guides my action toward the objects I see and hear in ways that would not be supported just by the ideas picked up from perception. So perhaps I yell in the direction of David Israel, "Hey, Paul Newman! Love your movies! Love your spaghetti sauce! Love your popcorn!"

To return to the Dretske case. What happens when Dretske says, "I wrote *Knowledge and the Flow of Information*"? My perceptual buffer is enriched by the idea that this fellow, the one I am talking to, wrote the book (he doesn't seem like the sort to fib about such a thing to a stranger at a party). Activity ensues on my mind's second story: perceptual plug finds notional socket. Information flows in both directions. This information is integrated with other things I know, including the social rule that one doesn't blabber on about a book to its author as if one knew all about it. I am embarrassed and turn red. I say something like, "Oh, I'm very pleased to meet you. I didn't recognize you. As you can tell I admire your work. I'm somewhat embarrassed." I shake his hand.

These remarks of mine, and my embarrassment, and my endeavor to shake his hand, seem to be explained by a new belief, a new bit of knowledge. It is what I shall call *recognitional* knowledge, the sort of knowledge that occurs when one attaches percept and notion. But what exactly is known in these cases?

6.2   Reflexive Contents

Consider now three of my mental states before recognition. One is my belief that Fred Dretske wrote *Knowledge and the Flow of Information*. On my simple model, this consists of my idea of being the author of *Knowledge and the Flow of Information* being belief-associated with my Fred Dretske notion. The second is my desire to shake Fred Dretske's hand. This consists of the idea of my shaking hands with a person being desire-associated with my Dretske notion. The third is my perception that the man in front of me is friendly and outgoing. This consists of my perception of Fred Dretske, attached to a perceptual buffer, which is associated with the ideas of being friendly and outgoing.

If we look at the way we use the concept "what is believed" or "what a person believes," we would find some good evidence for a referentialist treatment of beliefs about individuals, just as has been found in the case of statements about individuals using names, indexicals, and demonstratives (Barwise and Perry 1999, chap. 10; Crimmins and Perry 1989). A referentialist semantics takes the content of a statement to be a "singular proposition," that is, a proposition about the things referred to by indexicals and demonstratives, as opposed to one about identifying conditions somehow associated with those terms. In this case, we get the result that I want to shake Fred Dretske's hand and believe that Fred Dretske is standing in front of me, friendly and outgoing. Given this description of my mind, it is hard to understand why I don't reach out and grab his hand and give it a good shake: I want to shake x's hand; I believe x is standing in front of me; I believe x is friendly and outgoing.

The reason, in terms of our simple model, is that to activate that bodily movement that is a way of shaking hands I need to desire to shake the hand of the person in front of me. I would form that desire, as a way of fulfilling my long-standing desire to shake Dretske's hand, if all my beliefs about Dretske were in the same file. But they are not. There are two notions involved, my long-standing Dretske notion and my perceptual buffer. So I don't move.

Once I recognize Dretske, I do move my arm towards him, smile, and say, "I'd like to shake your hand"—a well-known procedure for shaking the hand of the person in front of one. *This action is rationally motivated by my new beliefs, in a way that it was not by my old.* Given the content of my beliefs, if my beliefs are true, this action is a way of satisfying my desire. But the subject matter content of my beliefs has not changed. We must reject the subject matter assumption and develop a richer concept of content to understand what is going on.

Consider two beliefs that I'll call b_1 and b_3. Belief b_1 is the one that I had before the party and would have expressed with (1). Belief b_3 is the one I acquired when Dretske said, "I wrote *Knowledge and the Flow of Information.*" As above, I'll assume that a belief about an individual involves a notion of the individual and ideas of the relevant properties and conditions.

The first belief, b_1, is not attached to my perception of Dretske. This sort of belief is (in more or less normal cases) about the *origin* of the notion: whoever or whatever it was that referred to in the information that established it. If things go right, the origin will also be the *source* of a vast majority of ideas associated with the notion.[15] In this case, the name "Fred Dretske" on the cover of *Seeing and Knowing*, the first book I read of his, referred to Dretske and led to my forming my notion. So it is a notion of him. The belief b_1 is true if that person wrote *Knowledge and the Flow of Information*.

The other belief, b_3, also involves a number of ideas associated in a file. But this file is attached to a perception. Information gleaned from the perception is put directly into the file. Information in the file is used to deal with the object being perceived. This sort of belief is about the individual who is perceived.

As I said, our ordinary concept of "what is believed" assigns contents in a way analogous to those the standard semantics assigns to statements (1) and (3). This referential semantics for beliefs will say that what is believed is a proposition about the individual the notion or buffer is of. My old notion, involved in belief b_1, is *of* Dretske, and so what is believed is that Dretske wrote *Knowledge and the Flow of Information*. My new perception is also *of* Dretske, and so what I believe after the recognition occurs is just what I believed before, that Dretske wrote *Knowledge and the Flow of Information*. This level of content doesn't give us what we need to understand what changed.

But there are many other levels available. I call the theory I favor the "reflexive-referential theory." I see it as growing out of the ideas of Hans Reichenbach (1947) and Arthur Burks (1949), as well as the work of figures like Kaplan, Donnellan, and Kripke (see Perry 1997a, 2001). Our ordi-

nary concept of content has had its critics, but I am enthu-
siast. Content is a way of classifying cognitive and linguistic events by their truth conditions (and success conditions
more generally). It is a key element of folk psychology, probably humankind's greatest intellectual accomplishment. We
need not to jettison content but to discover more of it, which
I propose to do with a formula I call the "content analyzer":

CA: Given *such and such*, ϕ is true iff *so and so*.

Here ϕ is any truth-evaluable representation, *such and such*
are facts about the representation, and *so and so* is the content assigned to ϕ given those facts. So and so is what *else*,
in addition to such and such, has to be the case for ϕ to be
true. If we vary what is given, we vary the content assigned.
These will not be different theories about *the* content of ϕ.
They will be ways of getting at different systematically related contents of ϕ.

I take the work of Kripke, Donnellan, and others on names
and Kaplan and others on indexicals to show that our ordinary concept of content is what I'll call "referential content."
If I tell my wife, "You are standing next to Dretske," we take
me to have expressed the proposition that is true if she is
standing next to him. It is true in worlds in which she is
standing next to him, whether or not I am talking to her (and
so in a position to refer to her with "you") and whether or
not he is named "Dretske" in those worlds. We are taking the
meaning, including the referent of the name "Dretske," as
fixed and taking the context as fixed. I shall say we are *loading* those facts. Given that the words mean what they do and
refer to whom they do, what else has to be the case for my remark to be true? My wife, Frenchie Perry, must be standing
next to Fred Dretske.

Now consider Donnellan's famous example, "The man
who murdered Smith is insane." As Donnellan points out,

there are two contents we might take such a statement to have. The first fixes the facts of reference but not the facts that fix the denotation of the description. Given that the statement is in English, the facts about its syntax and the meanings of its words, and the facts about the reference of "Smith," what *else* has to be the case for the statement to be true? There must be a unique individual that murdered Smith, and that individual must be insane. Suppose we add to what is given the fact that Jones murdered Smith, the fact that fixes the denotation of the description. Then what *else* must be the case for the statement to be true? Jones must be insane.

One can debate whether the first content, with the denotation allowed to vary, or the second, with the denotation fixed, is the proposition expressed by the statement. I'm not really interested in that debate for the purposes of this book. The point is that there are two contents, each of which may be useful for various purposes. If we want to explain why someone who heard the statement learned that Smith had been murdered, we would want the first content. If we want to explain why someone registered agreement by pointing to Jones and saying, "Yes, he is insane," we will want the second. We don't have to decide which content is "what is said." Both contents are simply there; each is a truth condition of the statement, taking certain things as fixed and allowing others to vary.[16] What we load and what we allow to vary depends on what is relevant.

What is not loaded remains relevant. Think of contents as propositions, and propositions as sets of worlds. In the worlds that are members of the denotation-unloaded content of "The murderer of Smith is insane," various people will murder Smith, and each of them will be insane in that world. The issue of murdering Smith remains connected to the issue of being insane. So this content is what we want when we explain how someone, by hearing the statement and understanding it, learned that Smith had been murdered.

On the other hand, *what is loaded ceases to be relevant.* If we take it as given that Jones murdered Smith, we have the denotation-loaded content. Given that Jones murdered Smith, what else has to be true for Smith's murderer to be insane? Jones has to be insane. In each world in the denotation-fixed content Jones is insane, but he need not murder Smith in all of them, and in fact nobody has to murder Smith; Smith does not even need to exist. The facts about Smith and his murderer are used to get us to Jones and then in effect thrown away. They are no more relevant to the truth of the denotation-loaded content than that the utterance was in English or that it occurred at all. The denotation-loaded content won't be of any use in explaining how someone came to know that Smith was murdered by hearing the statement. But it may be quite useful in getting at what is common between quite different statements in which Jones is referred to in quite different ways (see Burks 1949).

In fact, only a small part of the truth-conditions of an utterance are usually incorporated into what we think of as its content. The other parts are taken as given and exploited to get us to the subject matter we are interested in.

All of the contents we have looked at so far, including both denotation-varying and denotation-fixed contents of "The murderer of Smith is insane," are *subject matter contents*. They are the contents we get when we take the basic semantical relations between language or thought and the world as given on the left-hand side of the content analyzer. In the denotation-unloaded reading we take the the connections between property terms and properties, descriptions and

identifying conditions, the reference of names and the contextual facts that fix the reference of indexicals all as given.
For the denotation-fixed reading we take that as given and
also fix facts about the denotations of descriptions. Note that
on either subject matter content, we get propositions that
we can evaluate as true or false in possible worlds, *without
worrying further about the interpretation of language or thought
in those worlds*. We have loaded all the facts we need about
the utterance, so that the additional truth-conditions involve
only the subject matter.

Consider my statement (3). On the standard semantics for
indexicals and demonstratives, I would be taken to express
the singular proposition that Fred Dretske is the author of
Knowledge and the Flow of Information (Kaplan 1989). This
means we load the fact about whom I am demonstrating
into what is given. As our content analyzer puts it:

Given *that (3) is in English, etc., and given that the speaker is attending to and drawing attention to Fred Dretske, (3)* is true iff
*Fred Dretske is the author of Knowledge and the Flow of Informa-
tion.*

The fact that we take this content to be "what is said," however, does not mean that other, less-loaded contents are not
available. If we do not load the facts about context, we get:

Given *that (3) is in English, etc., (3)* is true iff *the person the
speaker of (3) is attending to and drawing attention to is the
author of Knowledge and the Flow of Information.*

This content is *not* a subject matter content. (3) itself is
not part of the subject matter of (3). I did not say anything
about my own utterance. But here we have not loaded the
contextual facts that get us from the utterance to the subject

matter. The utterance remains relevant. We have the truth conditions given as conditions on the utterance itself, or, as I shall say, we have *relexive* truth conditions for (3).

The context-unloaded contents of (2) and (1) are quite different from that of (3):[17]

Given *that (2) is in English, etc., (2)* is true iff *the person the speaker is addressing with (2) is the author of Knowledge and the Flow of Information.*

Given *that (1) is in English, etc., (1)* is true iff *the person the speaker of (1) is using "Dretske" to refer to is the author of Knowledge and the Flow of Information.*

These differences are useful in understanding the different motivations one would have for uttering (1), (2), or (3) and the different information one might pick up from hearing them. These differences disappear at the level of subject matter content, which is typically not very useful for explaining the cognitive significance of statements (see Perry 1993, passim).

As in the case of (3), our unloaded contents for (2) and (3) are *reflexive,* in the sense that the contents have the utterance themselves as constituents. I distinguish between *reflexive* content and both kinds of subject matter content.[18] Our own utterance is not usually part of what we are talking about, not part of the subject matter. Nevertheless, the reflexive content, the truth-conditions our content analyzer gives us when we do not take the contextual facts as given, is essential in understanding the motivation for making the statements and what is involved in understanding them.

Let's now return to b_1 and b_3. In these cases, too, we distinguish between reflexive contents and subject matter

contents. Notice that the issue here is not indexicality. Indexicality is a linguistic phenomenon: the rules of language
tell us that what certain expressions stand for depends on
contextual features. Here we are talking about notions and
ideas and their contents and causal roles, not expressions
in a language and the conventions that govern them. The
analogue to indexicality is the operation of the first-floor
ideas, the buffers that collect information about things that
play certain roles in our life, such as the object we see, the
object we touch. On my view this includes the self-notion:
the object we are identical to (Perry 1990, 1998). Indexicals are communicative devices; there are a relatively few
of them connected to fairly common communicative situations. Buffers are devices for the pickup, processing, classification, and application of information; they are ubiquitous
in our mental lives and have no particular connection with
communication. Indexicals are connected with a few common linguistic roles: buffers with all sorts of cognitive roles
(see Perry 1997c).

If we do not take the links between ideas and subject matter as given, we can "retreat" to reflexive truth-conditions in
the case of beliefs and other mental attitudes, just as we can
with language. The belief b_1 involves a notion that is, in fact,
of Dretske. When we set that fact aside, its truth-condition
is simply that whoever that notion is of wrote *Knowledge and
the Flow of Information*. Belief b_3 involves a perceptual buffer
that in fact is also of Dretske. If we set that fact aside, the
truth-condition is that whoever that perceptual buffer is of
wrote *Knowledge and the Flow of Information*. Dretske is not
a constituent of either of these propositions. The one has a
notion as a constituent, the other a perceptual buffer.

Just as the reflexive contents of our statements made clear
how two statements with the same subject matter content

can have quite different cognitive significance, the reflexive contents of our beliefs make clear how they can have different causal roles, each appropriate to its own reflexive content. Reflexive content is the level of content at which the belief's capacity, or lack of capacity, for motivating action is relevant. It is the level at which perceptual buffers, which guide local contributions to the results of actions, are relevant. It is the level at which knowing-that meets knowing-how, as we shall see in the next chapter. I know how to shake the hand of someone in front of me whom I am perceiving. I stick out my hand toward the person while smiling and perhaps saying, "I'd like to shake your hand," the fine movements being guided by the perceptions of my hand, the person, and their relationship. What ultimately drives the operation is a desire that will be satisfied only if I shake the hand of the person whom my present perception is of. That is, the ultimately motivating desire is attached to a perception of the person. This desire will typically be a subsidiary desire, formed in virtue of a belief that has as its reflexive content that the attached perception is of someone concerning whom I have a third-story desire.[19]

In the Dretske case, once recognition takes place, I form such a desire. When recognition takes place, my perceptual buffer and my notion share ideas. This includes not only belief-associated ideas but also desire-associated ideas. So the desire to shake a person's hand becomes associated with my perceptual buffer of Dretske. The subject matter content of this new desire is simply to shake hands with Dretske, the same as the subject matter content of the desire I have had for years. There is no change in subject matter content to explain why suddenly, after all of these years, I stick out my hand. This is explained by the change in reflexive content, however.

6.3   The Search for Recognitional Knowledge

Have we then found what we are looking for, the bit of knowledge that I gained when I came to identify Fred Dretske? Does this recognition amount to my believing something like the following?

(4)   The person that the perception attached to b_3 is of is the author of *Knowledge and the Flow of Information*

That is not the right way to look at it. One can see this in a couple of ways. In the first place, it would be a very odd belief for me to have. Well, that isn't quite right. After all we are dealing here with a philosopher talking to a famous epistemologist. I might very well be thinking about my beliefs and perceptions. I might be obsessing over them. Who knows what philosophers might be thinking about at parties. But at least it would be a very odd belief for most people to have.

Second, notice that believing the proposition in question would not guarantee that I am in the mental state we are after. Suspend your suspicion that I am making up a story about not recognizing Dretske. Assume I am telling you the literal truth. In that case I have told you about a belief I once had, b_3. You know quite a bit about it. And in particular you know (4), that the person that the perception attached to it is of is the author of *Knowledge and the Flow of Information*.

There is an important difference between

- believing a proposition P, and
- having a belief a reflexive content of which is P.

In general, the propositions we believe, the ones referred to by the phrase "what he believes," are not ones about our own perceptions and ideas but ones about their *subject mat-*

ter: the things, people, places, and events that our perceptions and ideas are *of*. That is, when we describe our beliefs and perceptions we standardly do so in terms of their subject matter contents. We do not say that I believe, of my Dretske notion, that it is of someone who wrote a certain book, but that I believe that Dretske wrote the book. But those very same beliefs have *other* contents that our content analyzer can get at by taking less as given. These are not alternative things the agent believes; they are less loaded contents of his belief.

It is important not to confuse the reflexive contents of statements about things with "metalinguistic" statements. A metalanguage is a language for talking about expressions of some object language. Statements in the metalanguage have the expressions of the object language as their subject matter. "Metalinguistic theories" of various statements maintain that statements that don't seem to be about language really are. Such theories are usually not correct.

Consider:

(5)   I'm Fred Dretske (said by Dretske).

This statement has Fred Dretske and identity as its subject matter. The subject matter assumption makes it puzzling (to philosophers with a sufficiently refined capacity for puzzlement) how Dretske can use this statment to convey his name to someone he meets. He does not say anything about his name. Why is Dretske's interlocutor able to learn his name from this statement but not from "I'm me"? The answer is that the fact that Dretske is named "Fred Dretske" is one of the statment's reflexive contents. We load the contextual fact that the speaker is Dretske but not the fact that "Fred Dretske" stands for Dretske. If Dretske is speaking to me, I'll be aware that the he is the speaker. Given that, his statement can only be true if he is named "Fred Dretske." Even though he doesn't mention his name but uses it, I learn his name.

Now consider

(6)   I'm named "Fred Dretske" (said by Dretske).

The subject matter content of (6), which refers to or mentions Dretske's name but does not use it, is the same as the crucial reflexive content of (5). But the subject matter contents of the two statements are not the same.

A truly metalinguistic theory of how (5) works would maintain that it really amounts to (6). This is not what I am claiming at all. After all, (6) also can be puzzling to us refined philosphers, but for a different reason. For how do we manage to figure out what to call Dretske from (6)? The subject matter content doesn't really explain this either. It is the same as the subject matter content of

Fred Dretske is named "Fred Dretske"

or of

Fred Dretske is named #Redfay Retskeay#,

which uses the metalinguistic device of naming an expression by enclosing its exact transcription into Pig Latin between # signs. We need reflexive contents to understand how (6) works. With neither (5) nor (6) do we get an explanation of the interlocutor's learning what to call Dretske from the subject matter content; in both cases we need to appeal to reflexive contents. I leave constructing an account for (6) as an exercise to the reader, but it is not required if the reader will simply promise not to call my account "metalinguistic."

Reflexive content itself may still be a bit mysterious, however. When we ascribe a belief to a person about a certain individual and involving a certain property or relation, we suppose that the agent has a notion of that individual and an idea of that property or relation. The agent keeps track of what is going on in the world in terms of those notions and ideas. But typically the agent will not have notions and ideas of all of the objects, properties, and relations involved in the reflexive contents. A person who had never heard of perceptions and had no idea that he had any could have a belief with (4) as its reflexive content. But then we might ask: what relevance can this content have to understanding our beliefs?

6.4   Information Games

Although the nonphilosopher of the last paragraph may not know about perceptions, he will know the difference between things he has perceptions of and things he does not. Moreover, he will be able to adjust his action to the nature of his perceptions; he will be attuned to the difference between having a perception of a man two feet away and one of a man three feet away, for example. In general, to be attuned to factors in a situation, you do not need all of the concepts that the theorist needs to discuss those factors. Attunement and belief are different kinds of doxastic attitudes toward situations.

It may be helpful here to introduce the concept of an "information game" (Perry 1997c). An information game involves two events: the pickup of information about something in the external world and the use of that information to guide behavior toward that thing in pursuit of goals. I see a tennis ball coming toward me, and I adjust my arm and wrist so that my racket hits it. This is an example, more or less, of a "straight-through" information game; I use the information I am picking up perceptually to guide almost simultaneous action. My action needs to be attuned to the nature of my perceptions. Beliefs don't have much to do with it.

Much of our lives is spent playing species of a quite different information game, however, which I call "detach and recognize." We pick up information about something in the external world at one time by having perceptions of it. We store that information away for later use. At some later time we recognize the object and use the information gotten previously to guide our behavior toward it. This approach doesn't work very well for playing tennis. But it works well with relatively stable properties of people, things, and places that we encounter over and over in our lives. I think the natural home for our concept of belief is to describe the information and misinformation we store in this detached way.

Suppose for example at the same party where I make a fool of myself with Fred Dretske, I also meet Krista Lawlor. Krista Lawlor is a young philosopher I have not previously heard of. When I meet her, a notion is assigned to store information about her. At first this notion is a perceptual buffer. I associate with it ideas of her interests, her name, her appearance, and so forth. But then the party ends. She goes one way, I go another. My notion is detached. We can suppose that the perceptual buffer is promoted to the third floor, or we can suppose that it sends all of its information up to a third-floor notion and then expires. At any rate, I go home with a detached notion of Lawlor.

If the file associated with this detached notion has enough relevant information in it, the next time I see Lawlor it will be helpful in two ways: in recognizing her and in acting appropriately. First, my memory of her appearance will help me to recognize her. My memory of her name will enable me to greet her in an appropriate way, by saying "Hi, Krista" instead of "Hey you" or "mumble-mumble." And my memory of her interests will enable me to engage in a mutually interesting philosophical conversation about, say, how we know when we have beliefs about the same thing, rather than merely saying "Nice weather" or "Read any good books lately?"

When we play the detach-and-recognize information game, the person who picks up the information and the person who applies it need not be the same, for the information may have been communicated from one to the other. This sort of information can be tremendously useful. I am heading to Bonn, Germany. I have never been there. I buy a map and a guidebook. They each provide, in different forms, information that I can attach to *my* perceptions of Bonn when I get there and then use to find the Opera House, or the university, or Beethoven's birthplace, or the McDonald's.

When we think of *knowledge*, we usually think of these detached representations—the representations that are capable of being passed from individual to individual, stored in libraries, perhaps for centuries, and then, at least in many cases, reattached to new perceptions of the relevant objects. And this leads to a central fallacy of philosophy, the fallacy behind the knowledge arguments and its cousins: the attempt to find attached knowledge in detached knowledge. It simply cannot be done. Search as he will, Terry will not figure out how to call Fran simply by using the phone book. Larry will not find out what day it is simply by studying the APA Bulletins. Gary will not figure out where he is simply by studying the road map. Useful knowledge, knowledge that guides our actions in pursuit of our goals, is attached. Detached knowledge is incomplete. The world of detached knowledge, the phone books and science books and libraries of the world, is the world of knowledge-completers. The view from nowhere is not a view at all. It is a mass of detached information, of no use until it is attached to a view from somewhere.

In the detach-and-recognize language game, attachments are used and then thrown away. I remember what Lawlor looked like, but I don't remember the perception I had. My cognitive structure is set up to keep track of facts about people, places, and things, not perceptions. They come, they do their job, they leave.

And thus when we characterize a person's belief and knowledge, we are typically after the detached knowledge. We ignore the shape of the connection between notion and thing. Just as our mind is set up to glean and retain facts about people, places, and things, our language for describing the mind focuses on the retained facts and not the means by which they were picked up or will be used. This is the reason subject matter content has such a robust life in folk psychology as what is said and what is believed.

But this is not always the case. We folk who use folk psychology are perfectly able to understand why I don't shake hands with Dretske until I recognize who he is—until I realize that he is Dretske. To understand the phenomenon of recognition one needs an enriched concept of belief content. One should think of a belief as having a hierarchy of contents, as more and more is taken as *given* and detached from the truth-conditions, culminating in the referential content. The other contents, the attributive and reflexive contents, are not different beliefs but different aspects of the same belief that can be characterized as attunements to more reflexive contents. These aspects that are necessary to understand the differences between beliefs with the same subject matter content and the changes that occur when we recognize and identify things.

Here, then, is my account of what happened when I identified or recognized Dretske. I did a acquire a new belief. This was a belief that involved my perceptual buffer coming to be associated with the idea of writing *Knowledge and the Flow of Information*. This new belief did not bring any new subject matter content with it, for its subject matter content was the same as my original belief, namely, that Dretkse wrote *Knowledge and the Flow of Information*. But its total truth-conditions are different than the belief I had before. It has different reflexive content. It is true only if the person my current perception is of wrote *Knowledge and the Flow of Information*. The reflexive content of this belief closes the gap between my desires and my action of extending my hand to Dretske. If my present perception is of the author of *Knowledge and the Flow of Information*, then the hand shaking directed by my present perception will be a way of shaking hands with the author of *Knowledge and the Flow of Information*.

6.5   Recognizing Universals

Concepts of universals—kinds, properties, relations, states, and so on—occur in our thinking in roughly three ways. First, we associate these concepts with notions of their instances. I think that Dretske is a philosopher; I associate my concept of being a philosopher with my notion of Dretske. Second, these concepts occur in general thoughts of various kinds: philosophers work hard for a living, philosophers are wise, philosophers are (sometimes) annoying, and so forth. Finally, we have thoughts in which the universal itself is the subject. Being a philosopher is a noble profession, the second oldest; it involves rational thinking and discussion about basic issues.

An ancient idea that still lives on in various ways[20] is that universals directly characterize the mind: the rose is red "formally"; when I look at it, my mind is red "objectively." A more plausible view is that our relation to universals is more direct than our relation to particulars; we know things *by* the properties they instantiate and the relations they stand in to other things. At the other extreme is the view that knowledge starts with particulars; knowledge of universals is gained by abstraction; perhaps universals are not as real as particulars, but simply classes of them, concepts that we use to think about them, or words we use as predicates for them.

I shall assume that universals are real, or at least as real as particulars (see Perry 1994), and that in the standard case they are known via sensations and concepts. Being red is one thing; my sensation of red is another thing; my concept of red is yet another thing. I think of red as a color, the color of blood, most fire hydrants, most ripe tomatoes, and pretty sunsets. It is associated with (and, according to Hilbert's [1999] persuasive arguments, identical with) the physical property of *reflectance*. It causes a certain kind of sensation that I have when I look at red objects in normal situations. I can use the same experience to attend to the sensation ("this$_i$ sensation") or the color ("that color").

Our concepts of universals are quite varied in structure. Many of my concepts of the kinds, properties, and relations of modern science are almost completely deferential. Quarks are whatever physicists say they are; spin is whatever scientists say it is; and so forth. I have no capacity to recognize a quark, or a case of spin, but I do have the capacity to recognize discourse in English about quarks and spin, and what material there is in my top-story idea of quarks and spin has gotten there via this route.

Other concepts of universals are highly deferential but contain a bit of theory and some recognitional elements: I can recognize some clear cases of steel and iron. I could go on for perhaps thirty seconds about the nature of iron and steel. There are volumes known beyond what I know. I *could* be wrong, even about my favorite skillet. It might be some kind of ersatz iron I can't tell from the real stuff, for all I really know.

Many of our concepts of sensible properties, such as being red, have a demonstrative/recognitional core. In normal daylight conditions most of us can simply look at a nearby object and say with great deal of confidence whether or not it is red. I'm likely to be more sure that a particular object I'm looking at is an instance of red than I am that almost any of higher-order properties that have made it into my concept of redness truly belong there. If I see a tomato or a fire hydrant that looks yellow and not red, I'll conclude that contrary to what I had thought, some fire hydrants and tomatoes are not red, rather than concluding that I was wrong about what red things look like.

Suppose now that you are demonstratively identifying the property of being red, pointing at a red object, and saying, "This color is red." If you are correct you have referred to the same property in two different ways. At the subject matter level, we can't get at the important cognitive differences between what you said and "This color is this color" or "Red is red." We can't explain, at that level, why what you said is useful for teaching someone the meaning of "red" or telling a color-blind person which color he is looking at. We can, however, use our content analyzer to get at various contents that do explain these things. First we fix the contextual facts relevant to your demonstrative phrase, but we do not fix the descriptive content of "red." Given that, your utterance can only be true if "red" stands for redness. This is what the first person above, who learns the meaning of "red" from your remark, grasps. If on the other hand we fix the descriptive meaning of red but allow the context to vary, the truth-condition is that the object you are attending to and pointing at is red. This is what the second person above learns.

Given the various kinds of information we have about universals and the various methods we use to recognize them, it should be no surprise that we can have complex concepts of universals, involving images, Humean ideas, typical instances, causes, effects, the expressions that stand for the universal, and so forth. We can have different concepts of the same universal, in much the same way that we have different notions of the same individual. These concepts can be unlinked; the identity of the universals they are concepts of can remain *unreflected* in the cognitive states of the subject. Imagine I am served a new dish, rosemary tofu with cranberries. The taste of rosemary is quite definite, but in this new context, I don't recognize it immediately for what it is. I may ask, "What is that taste?" I may hold the food in my mouth, savoring the new combination and trying to identify the herb. During that period I have a buffer of the taste of rosemary, tied to my current awareness of and attention to the sensation I am having, and a concept of rosemary, involving a grab bag of things, memories of past episodes of eating rosemary, recognitional abilities, the different kinds of rosemary plants I've seen, the smell of rosemary when burned in a barbecue, and perhaps the tune of the old Simon and Garfunkel song *Scarborough Fair* (containing the lyrics "parsley, sage, rosemary, and thyme"), and, of course, the noun "rosemary."

6.6   Recognition and Necessary Truth

I have just figured out that $33 = \sqrt{1089}$. This is a necessary truth. There are no possible worlds in which 33 is the square root of anything but 1089. How do we get at what I learned?

There is no straightforward way to do this in terms of eliminating possibilities. There are no possible worlds in which $33 \neq \sqrt{1089}$. So, there are no possible worlds to be eliminated from the ways I think the actual world might be.

We can abstract from the reference of one or both terms, re-treating to attributive truth-conditions. But merely abstracting from the reference won't help much, for the attributive conditions assigned by the meanings of the terms and the meaning of $\sqrt{}$ are rigid. Given the standard meanings, 33 refers to 33, and $\sqrt{1089}$ refers to 33, in every possible world.

We can retreat further, abstracting from the meanings, or part of the meanings, of some of the terms. This gives us some contingencies. For example, abstracting from the conventions that determine which specific numbers are assigned by the basic lexical conventions of decimal notation to "3," we obtain something like:

(7)   The number "3" stands for, added to the result of multiplying that number by 10, is the square root of 1089.

It seems wrong to say that this is what I learned by calculating the square root. But recall that this is not what we want to say on our account. The significant thing is that this is a reflexive truth-condition of the belief I acquired. We can say that what I learned is simply the necessary truth that $33 = \sqrt{1089}$. This is the content of my new belief. It was the consequence of things I already believed. But there is a big difference between being the reflexive content of a belief and being a consequence of the content of a belief.

Think of the sorts of situations in which one calculates a square root. The most obvious is on a math quiz, confronted with a question:

$$\sqrt{1089} = \underline{\qquad}$$

What one needs to answer the question is the ability to write in the correct numeral. If one has mastered decimal notation, then one knows that the way to write the numeral that "3" stands for multiplied by 10 and added to itself is to write "33." This ability is associated with a belief whose *reflexive* content is (7). When I calculated $33 = \sqrt{1089}$, I came to have such a belief. This was what changed about my beliefs. Of course I already knew that $33 = 33$ and that $\sqrt{1089} = \sqrt{1089}$; these beliefs are fully satisfactory from many points of view; they are both true, and both necessarily true, but they won't help you on the math exam, because their reflexive contents aren't what you need.

7 What Mary Learned

What then is Mary's *new* knowledge? The answer appears at the level of the reflexive truth-conditions of her beliefs. In this chapter I'll apply the account developed in the last chapter to Mary's case and argue that there is no problem for the antecedent physicalist. Then I'll compare my view to the views of Laurence Nemirow and David Lewis. Both argue that Mary's new knowledge is a case of knowing how *as opposed to* knowing that. Finally I will look at a discussion between Paul Churchland and Jackson that will enable us to see how the subject matter assumption underlies the knowledge argument. Just as epiphenomenalism is the real issue with the zombie argument, the subject matter assumption is the real issue with Mary. Those who hold it, dualist or physicalist, have a problem with Mary's knowledge. Those who reject it, dualist or physicalist, do not.

7.1 Mary's New Knowledge

Recall that the antecedent physicalist holds that there is a way of attending to a subjective character that is possible only when one is having an experience of which it is the subjective character. Attending to subjective characters in this

way and remembering having done so provides a demon-
strative/recognitional core, a Humean idea of the sensation
at the heart of many of our concepts of types of sensations.
There is a way of attending to delightful aspects of the experience of eating of chocolate chip cookies that is possible
only when one is having that experience. According to the
antecedent physicalist, this does not mean that the state of
enjoying a chocolate chip cookie is not a physical state or
that it could not be observed by others. Of course, there is
no reason to suppose that observing my delightful experience, perhaps by being a shrunken person trapped inside
my brain, would itself be particularly enjoyable.

When we are attending to a subjective character in the
subjective way and wish to communicate what we are feeling or noticing, we use our flexible demonstrative, "this," as
in "This feeling is the one I've been having." Let's label this
use of "this" as an inner demonstrative: "this$_i$." Mary could
use the following statement to express what she knew before
leaving the Jackson room, on the basis of her reading:

(1) Q_R is what it's like to see red.

and these statements to express what she learned upon seeing the ripe tomato:

(2) This$_i$ is what it is like to see red.

(3) Q_R is this$_i$ subjective character.

Let's call the beliefs expressed by (1), (2), and (3), b_1, b_2, and
b_3, respectively. According to the antecedent physicalist the
following can all be true:

• Q_R is a physical state, a physical aspect of the normal experience of seeing red.

(3) are true.

...ry leaves the Jackson room she learns something
...orming the new true beliefs b_2 and b_3, that she
...s with (2) and (3).

...s new knowledge is a case of recognitional or identifi-
...onal knowledge, as in the case with my new knowledge
...the party with Dretske. We cannot identify what is new
about it with subject matter contents; we can with reflexive
contents. Let's look closely at b_1, b_2, and b_3.

The reflexive truth-conditions of b_1, the belief Mary had in
the Jackson room and expressed with (1), are:

b_1 is true iff the origin of Mary's Q_R concept, the concept
involved in b_1, is the subjective character of the experience
of seeing red.

b_1 was a detached belief when Mary formed it from reading
a book; it never was connected to an act of attending to a
subjective character. It is analogous to my first belief about
Dretske, which existed for years before I had the opportunity to perceive Dretske himself and which was connected
to Dretske though a chain of communicative links. So too
Mary's concept is the end of a chain of communicative links;
she formed the concept reading about Q_R in a book; the
chain goes back to those who introduced the term, some of
whom will have done so on the basis of being subjectively
aware of the sensation of red.

The belief b_2 is analogous to my belief after Dretske introduced himself. That belief was attached to a perception of
mine, which was of Dretske. Mary's b_2 is attached to an act
of attention, which is of a certain subjective character. The

subject truth-conditions of (2) are exactly the same as thos
of (1). The reflexive truth-conditions of b_2 are different:

b_2 is true iff the act of inner attention to which it is attached
is of the subjective character of the experience of seeing red.

Finally we come to b_3. This is the belief Mary expresses
with (3), and it is the belief that Jackson found problematic.
It is a belief about what people in general experience when
they see red things, and it seems like the sort of thing she
should have known in the Jackson room, if she really knew
all of the physical facts about color and color perception. The
subject matter content of (3) is the same as that of (1) and (2).
But the reflexive content differs:

b_3 is true iff the act of inner attention to which it is attached
is of the origin of Mary's Q_R concept.

This is the new truth-condition on Mary's beliefs that results from the change that occurred when she saw the tomato and learned what it was like to see red. As in the cases
of Larry, Gary, and Terry, the change in Mary's beliefs does
not result in any new conditions on the truth of her beliefs
given what they refer to. But it does impose new conditions
on the truth of her beliefs *abstracting* from what they refer to:
the condition that the subjective character that is the origin
of her old concept is the very one to which she is attending.

That's my account of what Mary learned. But let's pause
for a moment to make another point, while Mary's situation
is before us. Take Mary back to the Nida-Rümelin room for a
moment. While there she had two concepts of the sensation
of red, Q_{wow} and Q_R. They were unlinked. Note that it would
have been perfectly coherent for her to have supposed, at
that time, that

(4) Q_{wow} is not Q_R.

The subject matter content of (4) is a contradiction. Since Q_{wow} and Q_R are one and the same subjective state, and there is no possible world in which that one thing is not identical with itself, (4) cannot be true. But the reflexive content of (4) is a contingent proposition, roughly that the subjective character that Mary experienced when she looked at a certain part of the plaid wallpaper, and of which she has certain memories, is not the same as the one that is the origin of the concept she acquired in the Jackson room. We can say that (4) is conceivable for Mary, when she is in the Nida-Rümelin room, because its reflexive content is consistent with the reflexive truth-conditions of her beliefs. When Mary takes her next step and sees the ripe tomato and her beliefs change as above, she will realize that

(5) Q_{wow} is Q_R,

since she will recognize that the color wow is the color red. At that point, (4) will no longer be conceivable for her. That is, the space of what is conceivable for Mary will have changed as a result of her new knowledge. What is conceivable for Mary now coincides with what is possible. Notice that there is no way Mary could have taken this step a priori.

   To review. The antecedent physicalist holds that the subjective characters of experience are physical aspects of experiences, to which we are able to attend when we have those experiences in a way that we cannot do when we do not have them. Given that subjective aspects are physical aspects, they can be in principle observed, discussed, and written up in textbooks. So people can learn about subjective characters that they have never had. They can know, of subjective characters they have never experienced, that they are the subjective characters normally associated with certain kinds of experience, such as seeing red. All of this does not mean that the antecedent physicalist needs to deny that a person in this position, such as Mary, learns something new when she does finally experience the subjective character in question. The new knowledge, as in the case with recognitional and identificational knowledge generally, is found at the level of reflexive content.

7.2 What Mary Remembers

Mary's experience will leave its trace on her concepts of red and of the sensation of seeing red. Having had the impression, she will have the idea and a cluster of recognitional abilities. The change is in her concept, in how she thinks of Q_R, not in what she thinks about. Suppose she now anticipates seeing the fire truck her mother drives. She has known all along that it is red. She has often had the thought, "Mother's fire truck is red." Now that she has experienced red, it seems that her belief has changed in important ways. During the time when she has no sensation of red, however, we cannot appeal to her sensation of red to explain the difference.

Let's call Mary's Humean idea of her sensation of red I_R. So we have an idea, I_R, which is an idea *of* (in Hume's sense) a sensation, Q_R, which in turn is a sensation of a color, red. Mary's concept of red has long included the fact that it causes Q_R. Before leaving the Jackson room, however, her concept of Q_R did not involve a Humean idea. Her concepts of red and of the sensation of red were both rather unusual, then, which was of course the whole point of keeping her in the Jackson room in the first place.

Consider Mary's thought, "Mother's fire truck is red," now that she is free. At the subject matter level, the truth-conditions have not changed from when she was in the room: the truck has to be red. But at the reflexive level, things have changed considerably. Let t be her mother's fire truck. Fixing the reference of "Mother's fire truck" but not fixing what her concept of red stands for, her idea I_R must meet the following condition for her thought to be true once she has had an impression of red, but not before:

$\exists s, c$ such that

1. s is a (type of) sensation.
2. c is the color of t.
3. s is of c.
4. I_R is *of* s (in Hume's sense).

We know Mary had an extensive concept of redness, based on her years of study in the Jackson room. So when she had the thought, "Mother's fire truck is red," while in the room, the truth of her thought put many conditions on the truck. It had to be the same color as tomatoes, it had to reflect and absorb various wavelengths of light, and it had to be of the color that caused Q_R. One thing not required of it, however, was to be of a color that caused a sensation of Mary's that gave rise to a Humean idea of hers. This was not part of the reflexive content of her belief. Now she has seen her tomato, had an impression, acquired an idea, and this further condition is required of the truck. Whatever else might be required of her mother's truck by the extensive concept Mary had of red before, it is now required to be of a color the sensation of which fits Mary's idea.

7.3   Recognitional Knowledge and Know-How

Laurence Nemirow has claimed, against the knowledge argument, that knowing what it is like is a species of knowing how (Nemirow 1979, 1980, 1989). According to Nemirow, Mary does acquire new knowledge, but it is not knowledge of a fact, hence not knowledge of a new fact, hence not an argument for nonphysical facts. It is a matter of know-how. Mary learns how to recognize red things by sight, how to recognize when she is having a red experience, and how to imagine seeing red things. Nemirow's ability analysis has been adopted and defended by David Lewis (1997), although there are differences in their positions, in that Lewis puts less emphasis on learning to imagine. There is a very close connection between know-how and reflexive knowledge. In this section I'll explore how Mary's new knowledge relates to her new know-how.

To discuss know-how, we need to develop a couple of concepts from the philosophy of action (see Israel, Perry, and Tutiya 1993; Goldman 1970). I'll use "act" for particular events and "action" for types. So acts involve an agent performing an action at some particular time and place. Actions I'll divide into *accomplishments* and *executions*. Executions are identified and individuated by the particular movements involved. Accomplishments are identified and individuated by the results they bring about. So by moving my fingers (executions) I bring it about that the keys on my computer are depressed (accomplishments). By bringing it about that the keys are depressed, I bring it about that the state of the computer changes in certain ways; by doing that I bring it about that letters appear on the screen, and so forth (more and more accomplishments). Action is a matter of executing movements that have results; intentional action is a matter of executing movements for the purpose of getting results; successful action is a matter of executing movements that get the intended results.

A given action, whether execution or accomplishment, may constitute a *way of* bringing about a result in certain circumstances. Depressing the keys is a way of making the letters appear on the screen *if* the computer is plugged in, the wires are intact, the right software is loaded, and so forth and so on.

For an action to be properly motivated by an agent's beliefs and a goal, the beliefs should close the gap between the action and the goal. That is, if the beliefs are true, the action should be a way of bringing about the goal. This will in general require two kind of beliefs: beliefs that in certain circumstances the action is a way of accomplishing the goal and beliefs that those circumstances obtain. My moving my fingers is motivated by my goal of making letters appear on the screen. I believe that moving the fingers is a way of making letters appear on the screen when the computer is plugged in, turned on, and working properly, and I believe that it is plugged in, turned on, and working properly. So my goal motivates my action.

Know-how is a special kind of knowledge of facts about "way-of" relations. (I'm also perfectly willing to talk about belief-how, which is a state that is internally like know-how, except the way-of relation doesn't hold.) A more natural way to say what I said in the last paragraph is that I know how to make letters appear on the screen if the computer is plugged in, and so on. But not every true belief about a way-of relation constitutes know-how.

To know how to ride a bike is to know which movements are a way of moving the bike in the direction you want to go without falling.[21] But not just any kind of knowledge of this will do. I may tell my wife, Frenchie, that if she simply turns gently in whichever direction she is starting to fall while continuing to look in the direction she wants to go, she will remain upright and can go wherever she wants. She may believe me. She may pass this information on to others. That doesn't mean she knows how to ride a bike. Know-how is a matter of attunement to a method, not possession of a formula describing the method. My granddaughter Anisa senses when her bike is falling in a certain direction, and turns gently into the fall while continuing to look in the direction she wants to go. She can recognize when she is doing this and when she is not; she can intend to do it and remember doing it. But she has no formula for describing what she does. Anisa knows how to ride a bike; Frenchie does not.

Let's identify a method for bringing about R with the fact that an execution of movements M is a way of bringing about R in circumstance C. Know-how is a positive doxastic attitude—that is, something belief-like, if not paradigmatically belief—toward a method in which the movements are represented in a way that the agent can execute at will in a broad range of circumstances. The representation of how the accomplishment is to be executed consists of the change that leaves the agent attuned to the way-of relation between the executions and the results, that is, that leaves the agent disposed to execute the required movements when he takes himself to be in the circumstances and intends to bring about the result. This means the agent may not be able to name or describe the actions but can perform them. Like Humean ideas, such executable representations are not always or even usually connected to words or descriptive abilities. And just as Humean ideas have an intimate and perhaps necessary connection to the impressions they are *of*, executable representations have a very intimate and perhaps necessary connection to the movements they represent.

I regard this condition of knowing how to do something as a species of factual knowledge. The fact that a certain type of execution will in certain circumstances be a way of bringing about a certain result is something that is internally represented, can be true or false, and is naturally regarded as a part of various concepts we have of various actions. Part of my concept of walking is that it done in a certain way, which I can demonstrate much more easily than I can describe. It is best to regard all of our knowledge as potential know-how; that is, our detached knowledge is of value only because in certain circumstances we can identify the objects it is about and will then know how to do things vis-à-vis those objects that we wouldn't know how to do otherwise. Recall the example of Krista Lawlor. I left the party knowing something about her: her name and some of her interests. The value of that was that combined with more basic know-how it enabled me, the next time I saw her, to greet her by name and ask something intelligent.

Thus there is a very close connection between recognition and know-how. Recognition extends know-how. When I realize that person A who plays role R in my life is also person B, then I learn that doing a certain thing to or for person A is a way of doing it to or for person B. I know how to talk to the person on the other end of the phone (talk into the end with the cord coming out of it). When I learn that you are the person at the other end, I know how to talk to you.

Suppose now that my sister Susan teaches me to make a certain aikido move, *tenchi nage* (the heaven-and-earth throw) perhaps.[22] I finally get the idea. I cannot describe it in words in any very coherent way. And I quickly forget the name. But I do remember how to do it. I can demonstrate it (in the living room, slowly) and actually do it (on the mat, with lightning speed). What makes this know-how is that I have an executable representation of the movements that are a way of performing the heaven-and-earth throw. This does not prevent it from also being knowing-that. I know that *this* (demonstrating the movement) is the way to do the heaven-and-earth throw.

Suppose that my cerebral but somewhat sedentary friend David, having read and memorized an aikido book, can give an excellent verbal description of the movements required for executing the heaven-and-earth throw but cannot perform it. He would have knowledge that a certain series of movements is the way to do the heaven-and-earth throw and know how to describe them but not how to do them. I know how to do them, but do not know how to describe them. But both of us have in our minds some representation of the movements; both bring the aikido technique in question under a concept. Mine is an *executable* representation, whereas his is not.

Note that David and I could *disagree* about the right way to execute the heaven-and-earth throw. He could (and no doubt would) object to my demonstration as faulty, based on his more descriptive and theoretical knowledge. I might tell him his description must be wrong. One of us will turn out to be right, the other wrong. If he is right, I didn't have know-how, but merely belief-how. Later I could go out on the mat, and say, "I thought *this* was the way to do the heaven-and-earth throw, but I was wrong, *this* is how you do it." I would be conveying what I learned from David.

We do things with our minds as well as with (the rest of) our bodies. There are mental actions we can execute at will—not very happily called "movements." One of them is attending to an experience we are having; another is trying to focus on what an experience is like so as to remember it; another is to focus on what it is like so as to recognize it. These are things we know how to do with respect to experiences that play a certain role in our life, that is, the ones we have. I can't focus on what the experience of seeing red is like if I'm not seeing red, any more than I can shake hands with Fred Dretske when he is in North Carolina and I am in California.

Consider Mary. When she is in the Jackson room, she knows a lot about Q_R. But she doesn't know how to imagine being in Q_R, she doesn't know how to recognize Q_R in the way most of us do, and she can't recognize red things in the way most of us do. When she finally sees the ripe tomato, she will gain that know-how. All this Nemirow points out, and he is correct.

Gaining all of this know-how may require a bit of effort on her part, however. I have seen puce many times and been told that it is puce, but I cannot now recognize puce things on sight, and I couldn't tell you if I was having a puce sensation or not. I need to focus on the experience of seeing puce the next time I have it. Perhaps it takes an unusually lazy person to notice the effort involved in such a simple thing; philosophy needs all types. Almost anyone who attends a wine-tasting seminar, to learn how to no longer be satisfied with wine he can afford, will find it takes effort and practice to discriminate among one's sensations in the way the experts do.

One key to learning to recognize sensations is to engage our memories and imaginations at the time we have the experience. There is a wide range of cases. Color sensations are probably among the easiest for normally sighted people to imagine, recognize, and remember names of. In the case of a smell, we are likely to be much better at remembering whether we liked it or not than being able to reproduce it in the imagination the way we often can with a color. In all of these cases, there seems to be a phenomenon of attending to the experience and noticing things about it, including one's own reaction, the situation in which it arises, and so forth. That is, it seems that one is bringing the experience under concepts, including concepts like "smells like *this*," where the "this" does not refer to the sensation or experience itself, but our reproduction of it in memory and imagination—not the impression, but the Humean idea.

The conception of knowledge I have developed exalts knowing-how in that it insists that complete knowledge is tied to buffers that are tied to ways of perceiving and ways of acting. In that context, it is easy to agree with Nemirow and Lewis that Mary's new knowledge is a case of knowing-how. I think, however, that knowing what it is like to have an experience and knowing how to do something are both special cases of knowing-that. They are special in that they involve special kinds of representations, Humean ideas in the one case, executable schemas in the other. So I do not agree with the negative part of Nemirow's account, that knowing what an experience is like is not a case of knowing-that.

Loar and Lycan give various persuasive arguments that count in favor of an account that treats knowing what it is like as a species of knowing-that, with propositional content. One is that Mary could have thoughts like "If apples hadn't looked like $this_i$, I would have found them more attractive." She can retain this thought in memory, thinking of the look in terms of the experientially based concept of what red things look like. Another is that we can apply our experience-based concepts of subjective characters to other people. Mary can wonder if Harry prefers the look of apples

to that of oranges, which she finds more attractive, because
he actually has the experience she has of red when he sees
orange (Loar 1990; Lycan 1995).

Nemirow emphasizes the connection between knowing
what it's like to have a certain sensation and gaining the
ability to imagine having the sensation. I'm inclined to think
that there is not much for us to disagree in about our positive accounts; I can think of what I say about Mary and
her knowledge as an extension of his positive account. Nemirow wants to insist that Mary doesn't learn a new fact
when she leaves the Jackson room, but he finds an epistemically relevant change in her. I adopt the two-ways strategy:
I say Mary knows an old fact in a new way, but I do find a
new bit of knowledge and a new fact at the level of reflexive
content. What I find in Mary's cognitive machinery doesn't
seem so very different from what Nemirow leaves there. So
it is not so clear that Nemirow would need to reject my account of Mary's new knowledge. It seems clearer, however,
that Lewis would.

7.4   Lewis and Eliminating Possibilities

In his essay "What Experience Teaches," David Lewis *de-
fines* "phenomenal information" as irreducibly nonphysical
(Lewis 1990, 583). Given this, he sees no hope for physicalism except to deny that there is phenomenal information.
He sees the ability hypothesis as the only alternative and
takes it to imply that phenomenal information is an illusion
(593). I think this approach is unfortunate, a sort of begging
the question against oneself. The antecedent physicalist simply identifies phenomenal information as whatever it is, if
anything, that Mary learns, and so on. That leaves us free

to explore the nature of phenomenal information and see whether it involves anything nonphysical and what its relations to gaining abilities might be.

The proposal I am putting forward seems to be an instance of what Lewis calls, a tad negatively, "the fifth way of missing the point." Lewis characterizes information in terms of eliminated possibilities. He says that there are conceptions of information that do not so characterize information. These conceptions foster "look-alike" hypotheses,

hypotheses which say that experience produces "information" which could not be gained otherwise, but do not characterize this "information" in terms of eliminated possibilities. These look-alikes do not work as premises for the Knowledge Argument. They do not say that phenomenal information eliminates possibilities that differ, but do not differ physically, from uneliminated possibilities. The look-alike hypotheses of phenomenal "information" are consistent with Materialism, and may very well be true. But they don't make the Knowledge Argument go away. Whatever harmless look-alikes may or may not be true, and whatever conception may or may not deserve the name "information," the only way to save Materialism is fix our attention squarely on the genuine Hypothesis of Phenomenal Information, and deny it.

The fifth way of missing the point involves appeal to the fact that Mary's mind has an internal structure of ideas for dealing with the world. Lewis assumes that appealing to changes in that structure to explain what goes on in Mary's case is simply to miss the point by appealing to an irrelevant concept of information. He uses the analogy of taking a course in Russian versus taking a course in English. "Each of the look-alikes turns out to imply not only that experience can give us 'information' that no amount of lessons can give, but also that lessons in Russian can give us 'information' that no amount of lessons in English can give (and vice versa)" (Lewis 1990).

The subject matter assumption is apparent in Lewis's discussion. Loar says, I think quite insightfully, "physicalists are forced into the Nemirow-Lewis reply if they individuate pieces of knowledge or cognitive information in terms of possible-world-truth-conditions" (Loar 1990). I would simply add that it is seeing the truth-conditions not in terms of possible worlds, but in terms of possible worlds that deal only with possibilities for the *subject matter*, that is the problem. To see the point, recall the discussion of Mary in the Nida-Rümelin room in section 7.1. It was conceivable for her there that Q_{wow} and Q_R were different subjective characters. It became inconceivable when she moved into the next room and saw the ripe tomato. What she learned cut down on what was conceivable. Of course, it did not cut down on what was possible, if we confine ourselves to the subject matter possibilities. But why should our conception of information be so inflexible as this? We'll return to these issues in the next chapter.

Let's consider Lewis's analogy for a moment. Suppose I am a native speaker of Russian, taking a course on cooking pasta that is given in English. If my English is perfect at the beginning and I have no knowledge of how to cook pasta, then we can characterize everything I learn in terms of the subject matter of the class. More likely, I know something about pasta and have a partial grasp of English. Suppose, for example, that I know that "vermicelli" and "linguini" are both names of varieties of spaghetti, and I have narrowed down the candidates for each to the same two varieties. Each of the two varieties I know how to cook perfectly. One kind you boil for four minutes, the other for six. I just don't know which name stands for which. In the course of the lessons, I will learn which variety each of the words stands for. This will eliminate possibilities, but they may not be subject matter possibilities. The teacher may have simply said, "Boil vermicelli only four minutes, not six." I eliminate the possibilities that "vermicelli" stands for linguini and "linguini" stands for vermicelli.

The line between learning about the meanings of English words and learning about pasta is not a line between two concepts of information, one having to do with the elimination of possibilities, the other having merely to do with the presence of syntactic structures of some sort. The line is between what we took to be the subject matter of the class and what we didn't. A class in English as a second language for Russian pasta cooks might involve the very same words from the very same teacher; there the official assumption would be that the students know what kind of pasta should be boiled for how long, not that they know the names used in English for the different kinds of pasta.

All of the contents that the content analyzer can find are contents that involve the elimination of possibilities. But the possibilities eliminated cannot all be represented as permutations of the subject matter. Jon Barwise liked to say that language is a balancing act. What we may learn about from a particular utterance may be the context (if this is true, who must have said it, and when must it have been said?); the language (if this is true, what does "vermicelli" stand for?) or the subject matter (if this is true, how long do you boil vermicelli?). If we forget this in looking at the knowledge argument, we will be caught between Jackson and Lewis, between misconstruing phenomenal information and ignoring it.

The Russian example actually brings out the close connection between reflexive knowledge and abilities. Courses given in English and courses given in Russian presuppose quite different abilities on the part of the students. For most of us, knowing the meaning of the words of a language is not a matter of explicit beliefs about the words and their meaning. Rather, we have the ability to hear sentences in the language, combine the reflexive contents with other information, and form explicit beliefs about the subject matter.

7.5   Churchland's Challenge

I want to end this chapter by looking at an exchange between Paul Churchland and Jackson that helps show that it is the subject matter principle that leads to the problem philosophers have with Mary. In the exchange, we see that Jackson thinks that physicalism is committed to this for some reason, whereas dualism is not.

Churchland tries a parity-of-reasoning argument to show that there must be something wrong with the knowledge argument. As Jackson summarizes Churchland's argument, "Suppose Mary received a special series of lectures over her black and white television from a full-blown dualist" that gave her all the facts about dualism and qualia. "This would not affect the plausibility of the claim that on her release she learns something. So if the argument works against physicalism, it works against dualism too" (Jackson 1997, 569, summarizing Churchland 1985).

Imagine that dualism is true. There is no reason that Mary can't read about this in her room. And there is no reason that the subjective character of seeing red things can't be called "Q_R" and information about it printed in black and white and given to Mary in her room. That is, imagine things are just as before, except that instead of being neutral between physicalism and dualism, the discussion of Q_R in Mary's texts emphasizes that it is not a physical state of the brain but some kind of nonphysical state.

Imagine that Mary, having read and believed all of this, comes out of her room and sees a fire hydrant or a ripe tomato. It seems that there would be a experience gap. Mary could still think, "Ah, so *this* is what it is like to be in a brain state with that nonphysical aspect I read about, the one that is involved in seeing red things, Q_R. There would still be a gap between Mary's reading about Q_R, and coming to know that it is the subjective character of the experience of seeing red, and having the experience. And it seems that as long as there is that gap, she learns something new when she has the experience. If it is a problem for the physicalist, shouldn't accepting dualism have eliminated it?

Jackson replies that there is no reason to believe that everything about subjective characters could be told to Mary in the black and white room. "To obtain a good argument against dualism . . . the premise in the knowledge argument that Mary has the full story according to physicalism before her release, has to be replaced by a premise that she has the full story according to dualism. The former is plausible, the latter is not. Hence, there is no 'parity of reasons' trouble for dualists who use the knowledge argument" (Jackson 1997, 569).

Let the brain state that we go into when people with normal vision see red objects in normal light be called S. Take Q_R to be an *aspect* of S. Call the fact that S has aspect Q_R, *that-S-is-Q_R*. If Q_R is a physical aspect of brain states, then *that-S-is-Q_R* is a physical fact. If Q_R is a nonphysical aspect of brain states, then *that-S-is-Q_R* is a dualist fact.

It seems that whether *that-S-is-Q_R* is a dualist fact or not, we can imagine Mary learning *that-S-is-Q_R* in the black and white room. She just reads a textbook, written by an authoritative person, that says something like

There is a certain aspect of some brain states, that one is immediately aware of when one is in them, that we call their subjective characters. They are extremely important and interesting. One of the most studied subjective characters is Q_R, which is the subjective character of the experiences that normal people have when they see bright red objects, such as fire hydrants or ripe tomatoes. For a long time it was not clear whether Q_R was a physical aspect of brain states or a nonphysical aspect, but now it is known that . . .

What is said up to the ". . ." would be agreeable, it would seem, to either an antecedent physicalist or a dualist. Once Mary reads that, she knows that Q_R is the subjective character of seeing red; that is, she knows *that-S-is-Q_R*.

In either case, even though she knows *that-S-is-Q_R*, it still seems that intuitively she will learn something when she comes out of the Jackson room and has the requisite experience of seeing a fire hydrant or a ripe tomato. There will be an experience gap. No matter how carefully she has read the above paragraph—even if she has read whole books on Q_R, even if she has written them—it seems she will still be able to say,

Oh, so this is what it is like to see red, that is, this subjective character is Q_R.

So it seems the experience gap has nothing to do with physicalism; Churchland is right, it is equally a problem for dualism and physicalism.

The problem is that the subject matter assumption sneaked into the Mary case with a apparently innocent remark we made in describing the Jackson room: *that if something was known, it could be written down in black and white and Mary could read it and learn it in the room.* When Churchland assumes the very same thing for dualism, the experience gap problem and the knowledge argument emerge as problems for dualism. And it is this step that Jackson says isn't fair: all physicalist knowledge can be written down, he implies, but not all dualist knowledge can be.

The real engine of the knowledge argument now comes front and center, and it is the subject matter assumption. The physicalist is assumed to be committed to something about objectivity that leaves him unable to admit that Mary gains new knowledge when she emerges from the Jackson room, knowledge one can gain only by having an experience. The dualist is not assumed to be precluded from recognizing this new knowledge. But there is no reason for these diverging assumptions.

The antecedent physicalist is committed to subjective ways of knowing physical facts in the following pretty clear and perfectly reasonable sense. There is a way of knowing what an experience is like that is available to a person who is having the experience that is not available to others. A sighted person can know what it is like to see objects in a way that a person who has never seen cannot.

Is there anything about this that violates the spirit of physicalism? I do not see that there is. All that is violated is a false picture of knowledge. This is the view that there is some kind of knowledge that involves grasping a fact not from any point of view—a view from nowhere. Knowledge consists of the subject matter fact known, and the way it is known is irrelevant: the perspective, the language, the sensory states, the particular system of ideas and notions don't matter.

This is a natural extension of the subject matter assumption. If the content of our beliefs is exhausted by the requirement their truth puts on their subject matter, then the methods of representation won't matter. The language won't matter, the context won't matter, and so forth. What is known will not constrain the knower to have any particular means of representation. Hence it will be possible to have any bit of knowledge by means of representations that don't "locate" the knower in any way. This means that the references will not be by means of any roles that the subject matter plays in the life of the knower. The subject matter won't be, relative to the knower, I or you, this or that, here or there.

But this is a false picture of knowledge. A system of objective representation is a system for completing knowledge and does not constitute the whole of knowledge. It would be, for us, like the phone book for poor Terry, two chapters back, who cannot get a date. True knowledge is knowledge only because of its potential for being attached to perceptions and actions. Terry won't get a date as long as all that Terry knows about the phone number is what Terry reads in black and white in the phone book. Physicalists need not find Mary's lack of knowledge in the Jackson room with the physics books memorized any stranger that Terry's lack of knowledge at the party with the phone book memorized. Physicalism should be no more opposed to qualia than it is to dating.

Science is supposed to be objective in several senses. Experiments should be replicable by different people in different laboratories. Observations should be public and verifiable. Results should depend on what is observed to happen in the experiments, rather than what a particular person, group, or funding agency wants to be true. And so forth. In science, as in all human communication, we seek an appropriate mode of representation. Scientific results should be published in a journal and in a language that many scientists have access to; new terms should be explained in this well-known language; and information should be conveyed in ways that do not require the reader to know details of the writer's situation or personal circumstances that are not supplied. All of this does not add up to any special commitment on the part of scientists in general or physicalists in particular to the subject matter assumption and the odd doctrine of objectivity it entails. Without the subject matter assumption, the knowledge argument is no more of a problem for the physicalists than it is for the dualists; with the assumption, it is a problem for both.

8   The Modal Argument

[I]t is downright self-contradictory to say (in a reasonably constructed and interpreted language) that Smith is Jones, or that I am you. The Mont Blanc cannot conceivably be identical with Mt. Everest!

—Herbert Feigl, *The "Mental" and the "Physical": The Essay and a Postscript*

The zombie argument we examined in chapter 4 is a modal argument. It is claimed that a something is possible, a world physically indiscernible from ours but with no consciousness. From the existence of a possibility, an inference is made about the actual world: physicalism is false. I maintained that the argument did not work against the *identity* theory of the antecedent physicalist, for the antecedent physicalist has no reason to grant the premise.

The first and simplest modal argument was advanced against such an identity theory, however, by Saul Kripke in *Naming and Necessity* (1997). Chalmers puts forward a somewhat similar argument. In this chapter I'll examine these arguments. I will argue that if we keep firmly in mind the lessons learned in chapters 6 and 7 about recognition, unreflected identities, and the subject matter fallacy, these arguments will be unconvincing. I will begin by making a few points about using possibilities, possible worlds, and possible-worlds semantics to get at our sense of what might be and what might not be.

8.1 Contents and Possibilities

Possible-worlds semantics models the subject matter truth-conditions of sentences as a first step toward modeling truth-conditions of more complex sentences involving operators for necessity, possibility, and other concepts. Expressions have intensions, which are functions from possible worlds to appropriate extensions. The intensions of names are typically functions from worlds to individuals; the intensions of n-place predicates are functions from worlds to sets of n-tuples; the intensions of sentences are functions from worlds to truth-values determined by the intensions of the parts. The proposition expressed by a sentence can usually be thought of as simply a set of worlds, the worlds for which its intension delivers truth. The proposition expressed by, say, "Elwood walks" is the set of worlds in which the intension of "Elwood" delivers an object that is in the set delivered by "walks." The worlds themselves can be thought of as indices for models of the language in question, or as concrete realities (David Lewis), or as abstract ways the world might be (Robert Stalnaker), or in various other ways, depending on one's purposes and one's metaphysics.[23]

This way of modeling truth-conditions of statements has led to considerable clarity about the logic of modality. Attempts to use the system for epistemic purposes, however, have been plagued by problems, many of which can be traced to the subject matter fallacy.

One matter that has been considerably clarified by the use of possible-worlds semantics, formally and informally, is the

issue of the necessity of identity. In the late 1940s and 1950s,
Ruth Barcan Marcus' systems of quantified modal logic fea-
tured the necessity of identity. By and large the reasons for
this were not appreciated by philosophers; indeed, this feature drew criticisms to her system (Marcus 1946, 1961). Until
Kripke's *Naming and Necessity*, advocates of the mind-body
identity theory typically claimed that the identity between
mind and body, and between particular mental states and
brain states, was *contingent*. Kripke argued forcefully and
persuasively that identity is always necessary. One thing
cannot be two things. What can happen is that two terms
can co-refer in one world but refer to different things in
other worlds. For example, Clinton was the president of
the United States at the turn of the century. But it is not
necessary that this be so; Clinton might not have been the
president of the United States at the turn of the century. This
sort of "contingent identity" can happen if the reference of
one or both of the terms depends on facts that vary from
world to world. In the example, "the president of the United
States at the turn of the century" refers to Clinton in the actual world, but not in worlds in which Dole won the 1996
election.

Proper names like "Bill Clinton" are *rigid designators*, according to Kripke. This means that they refer to the same
object in every possible world. If we have a true identity
with two rigid designators, then the proposition expressed
is necessarily true. For example, "Bill Clinton is Bill Blythe"
is necessarily true, for both names refer to the president.

A childhood friend of Clinton's in Arkansas, when he was
called "Bill Blythe," who now sees him daily on television
might fail to realize that Bill Clinton is Bill Blythe; he might
in fact think the whole idea was absurd. This particular false
belief cannot be modeled by the set of worlds in which it is

true, for there are no worlds in which it is true; it is necessarily false. Or, more accurately, it can be modeled by the null set of worlds, but that does not distinguish it from a lot of other necessarily false beliefs that the childhood friend doesn't have, such as that $7 = 5$ or that Hope, Arkansas, is Little Rock, Arkansas. What's worse, when the friend learns that Bill Blythe is Bill Clinton, the proposition he learns is the same as one he already knew, in virtue of knowing that Bill Clinton was Bill Clinton and Bill Blythe was Bill Blythe.

One might be tempted to draw the conclusion that possible worlds are not much good for getting at the contents of belief states. That is not the correct lesson, however; rather, it is that one needs to be careful in using possible-worlds semantics in getting at the content of belief states, since the more familiar forms of possible-worlds semantics are built to ignore all but subject matter content.

One might ask whether "Bill Clinton" is really a rigid designator. After all, there are worlds in which Clinton doesn't have that name and someone else does. But that doesn't count against rigid designation. Recall the principle of chapter 6 that what is fixed is not part of the content. In using the concept of rigid designation, we are thinking of the meaning of the expression as given, as fixed. Proper names are rigid designators because the linguistic conventions that constitute the meaning assign individuals to the name. The relevant rule might be conveyed by saying, " 'Bill Clinton' stands for that fellow right there," while pointing at Clinton. So, given this rule, what *else* has to be true for "Bill Clinton was born in Arkansas" to be true? That is, in what worlds will this be true? Those in which Clinton was born in Arkansas, whatever he is called in the world.

Possible-worlds semantics and concepts like "rigid designation" are oriented toward the subject matter truth-conditions of statements; to suppose that they can be used, without supplementation, to characterize belief and knowledge, including belief and knowledge about what is possible and what is not, is to commit the subject matter fallacy.

This does not mean that possible worlds themselves are useless in characterizing belief and knowledge. Suppose Clinton's boyhood acquaintance does not know that Clinton was born in Arkansas, although he does know that Bill Blythe was. How can this be so? The information flow analysis is pretty obvious. He has two notions, one acquired in interactions with Clinton as a boy, the other acquired from seeing Clinton on television. One notion is involved in his understanding of the convention governing "Bill Blythe," the other in his understanding of the convention governing "Bill Clinton." They are not linked. All of these facts can be usefully modeled with possible worlds. The possible worlds in question, however, need to deal with names, concepts, notions, utterances, and other paraphernalia of thought and language and not simply with the subject matter the thought and language are about.

The friend may be surprised when Clinton turns out to be Blythe; he may have bet a great sum that this would not be so; the fact that it is so may seem amazing to him; all of this in spite of the fact that it is a necessary truth that Clinton is Blythe. What fact is it that surprises him? Is it that the names stand for the same person? That his notions stand for the same person? That anyone from his hometown could be so important? That good old reliable Bill Blythe became a politician? There are a cluster of facts, some involving thought and language, some involving co-instantiation of properties flowing across the new link between the Clinton and Blythe notions, that account for the childhood friend's surprise and explain his willingness to bet against a necessary truth before the link was made. It is a mistake to try to localize the sense of contingency; the change that represents a crucial reflexive fact, such as the fact that "Clinton" and "Blythe" co-refer, leads to a flood of information that is full of surprises and can change one's whole view of the world, its future, the place of Arkansas in the scheme of things—all of this, even if the subject matter conditions of the belief are necessary.

Note that there are many contingencies involved in getting straight about even the most necessary of truths, say

MLXXXIX = 1089,

or

$$\sqrt{\text{MLXXXIX}} = \text{XXXIII}.$$

I might learn, from encountering the first in some reliable source, that L was the Roman symbol for 50 and not 500. Both conventions were possible choices for the Romans to make, and their possibility underlies my having been able to conceive that MLXXXIX might not be 1089.

I'll use the term "real possibilities" for subject matter possibilities and the terms "conceivable" and "conceivabilities" and "possibilities for so and so" and "possible for all so and so knows" in broader ways. Every conceivability is based in a real possibility about *something*, but it may be a possibility about some quite different subject matter than that of the thought or statement in question. It's not really possible that $\sqrt{\text{MLXXXIX}} \neq \text{XXXIII}$, because relations among numbers are matters of necessity; but it might be possible, for all I know, or conceivable, if I'm not sure whether L stands for 50 or 500. The real possibility that underlies my conceiving that $\sqrt{\text{MLXXXIX}} \neq \text{XXXIII}$ might be true is that L could have stood for 500. That's a real possibility about a symbol, not about 1089 or 33, the subject matter of my thought. The real possibilities that account for one's ignorance and one's sense of contingency are often not the subject matter contents of one's statements and thoughts but the reflexive contents.

In adopting the language of "real possibility" I fear granting, for the sake of argument, a little more than I am comfortable with. I think there is a cluster of views and concepts that derive from a certain picture that the theory of reflexive contents tries to shake off. The picture is of a fully interpreted language, with all of the semantical facts fixed, with which we communicate and think about the subject matter. What we really say, what we really know, the real possibilities that we are concerned with all concern this subject matter. Information about how our language or system of concepts and notions fits onto this subject matter is not quite knowledge; to think it is so is a "way of missing the point" (Lewis 1990) or a matter of mistaking knowledge of language for genuine knowledge (Frege 1892, criticizing his earlier theory). This picture of communication, knowledge, and possibility is perhaps an "ideal of semantics." I'll call it the "objective ideal." For the purpose of understanding our thoughts, it is a misguiding ideal.

The objective ideal cannot model even so simple a situation as my failure to know that $MLXXXIX = 1089$. To model it, we need to abstract from the connections between the symbols "MLXXXIX" and "1089" and the numbers for which they stand. When I learn that $MLXXXIX = 1089$, the *crucial fact* is simply that both symbols stand for the same number. If the subject matter assumption prevents our system from representing the key change, the change will remain a mystery. In Berkeley's phrase, we will have thrown up dust and then complained that we cannot see.

This point may be clearer if we step back and look at a larger issue. I think that knowledge and truth are a matter of correspondence to facts, in spite of all the energy wise philosophers have spent explaining the naïveté of this view.

When we know something, the ways the ideas in our head are connected corresponds to the way things are related in the world outside our heads. This view seems to support the ideal sketched in the last paragraph. If knowledge consists in having the relations among our ideas correspond with the relations among the things they stand for, it seems that having true subject matter contents is the goal, and the only information that moves us toward that goal will be the elimination of real possibilities. But the heads and ideas and connections to the subject in question are parts of the world represented. Forming beliefs on the basis of perception and using them in action requires that the connections between our ideas and notions and the object they are of be reflected in our cognitive system. We need knowledge that reflects not just the way things are among themselves, but also how they are *for us*, how the ideas in our heads are connected to the subject matter they represent. This is done by links between buffers, concepts, and notions.

At the risk of beating an old joke completely to death, recall once more our friend Terry from chapter 5, who wants the number of the person he or she talks to at a party. The phone book doesn't do Terry any good, even though it is all true, and even though Terry has memorized every name and number in it. It is knowledge, but it is not properly situated knowledge, and will not be, until this bit can be added: "That person is Fran Smith." To eliminate ignorance of the sort that Terry has, one needs beliefs whose *reflexive* contents place conditions on one's own perceptions and ideas. The ideas need to come into the content not as one more thing represented, but as the things the reflexive truth-conditions of the belief put conditions on. Terry needs to have a thought whose reflexive truth-conditions are that his perception is of a person with phone number 555-1234.

There is a tremendous focus on, and a thriving commerce in, what I sometimes call "completing knowledge." This is what the phone book will provide Terry, once Terry has the thought above to complete. Representations designed to serve as completing knowledge will put only rather general reflexive truth-conditions on statements and thought. In the metaphor of chapter 6, they are designed to stay at the third floor, and to be attached to the world, when relevant, via first-floor ideas, which will vary from time to time, place to place, or person to person. The ideal of objective knowledge and the focus on these relatively context-insensitive representations are two sides of the same coin. You can't represent what Terry wants to learn by modeling only the facts reported in the phone book.

Kripke and Chalmers both start from the premise that denying particular identities between brain states and sensations makes sense. There are no a priori arguments available to establish the identities and refute their denials. If we grant that the coherence of such thoughts establishes a real possibility of nonidentity, then there cannot be identity, for identity is a matter of necessity.

Suppose it is definitely established that the physical correlate of Q_R is B_{52}. A dualist thinks that no matter how well the states are correlated, B_{52} could occur without Q_R occurring. A physicalist could think it might have turned out to be B_{47} instead. The antecedent physicalist needs to provide some explanation of these thoughts. If the antecedent physicalist accepts the subject matter assumption and confines his search to the realm of real subject matter possibilites, he will not be able to find a contingency to explain the coherence of the thoughts and will have to accede to adding some subject matter to the physical world.[24] But the antecedent physicalist rejects the subject matter assumption and so has other places to look.

8.2   Kripke's Argument

Consider Q_R. Suppose its physical correlate has been identified. Many scientists, including Mary, as she published
articles while trapped in the Jackson room, thought that the
correlate was B_{47}, that is, the brain state with the scientific-
structural description that we will imagine to be conveyed
by "B_{47}." But in fact it turned out to be B_{52}. The antecedent
physicalist now claims that Q_R and B_{52} are one thing, one
and the same property or condition. If they are one thing,
then there is no way they can be two things, and there is no
possible world in which "they" occur separately. In maintaining identity, then, the antecedent physicalist maintains
necessary identity. So conversely, if there is such a possibility, Q_R and B_{52} are not one thing, and the antecedent
physicalist is wrong. Both modal arguments claim that there
seems to be such a possibility and that it cannot be explained
away.

Consider Mary while she believes that Q_R is *not* B_{52}. Her
belief seems coherent. But it is false. The natural explanation is that she believes something coherent, something that
could have been true, something that is possible. Both modal
arguments accept this natural explanation. I will argue that
this natural explanation is not the right one. Her thought
was coherent not because the subject matter content of her
thought could have been true but because the reflexive content of her thought could have been true. The subject matter
of her thought could not have met the conditions the truth
of her thought put on it, *given* the reference of "Q_R" and
"B_{52}." Her thought could have been true only in the sense
that "Q_R" and "B_{52}" could have referred in such a way that
her thought was true: her system of thought could have fit
into the world in a way that made it true.

Kripke focused on pain and assumed that the identity the-orist claims it to be identical with stimulation of C-fibers (Kripke 1997, 446ff). If this identity is true, it is necessary. There is just one thing, one property or state, that is both C-fiber stimulation and pain. This means that there could not be a C-fiber stimulation that was not pain, nor pain that was not a C-fiber stimulation. This is surprising, Kripke says, but not yet fatal to the identity theorist, for, perhaps the identity theorist can show "that the apparent possibility of pain not having turned out to be C-fiber stimulation, or of there being an instance of one of the phenomena which is not an instance of the other, is an illusion of the same sort as the illusion that water might not have been hydrogen hydroxide, or that heat might not have been molecular motion" (Kripke 1997, 447). In these cases, the key fact is that the designators "water" and "heat" are associated with shared public meanings that attribute certain properties to their designata. "Water" des-ignates H_2O because H_2O is what we find in our lakes and rivers and oceans, what we drink, and so forth. "Heat" des-ignates rapid molecular motion, because that's what makes fire cook things and what causes in us the characteristic sen-sation, the sensation of heat. Although it is not contingent that water *is* H_2O, it is contingent that H_2O is found in lakes, rivers, and oceans. Although it is not contingent that heat *is* rapid molecular motion, it is contingent that rapid molecu-lar motion causes the sensation it does. These sorts of facts give statements like "water is H_2O" and "heat is molecular motion" an "illusion of contingency."

One way to look at this is that there is a set of criteria as-sociated with our use of words like "water" and "heat." We use these criteria to say when we are encountering water and heat. Linguistic competence requires knowing the cri-teria, although they don't necessarily have to be the same

for everyone; for one thing, our criteria may involve defer-
ring to experts. But in the case of heat, say, the assumption
is that the we have a concept that includes various of the criterial properties of heat that have been known for centuries,
most importantly the property of producing its characteristic sensation. We may suppose, with Kripke, that kind terms
rigidly designate the underlying structures and processes
that account for the phenomena they are used to describe;
heat *is* rapid molecular motion and is so in every possible
world. But if we leave the reference of "heat" unfixed and retreat to the criteria that govern its application, we obtain the
contingent proposition that rapid molecular motion causes
the characteristic sensation. This accounts for the sense or
"illusion" of contingency that attaches to the thought that
heat is molecular motion. We can retreat from the subject
matter content to the criterial content to understand these
cases. In my terminology, the analysis of the water and heat
cases is a partial retreat from subject matter content.

The antecedent physicalist cannot account for the apparent contingency of "Pain is stimulated C-fibers" in the same
way. Pain is the sensation I am having, not the underlying
cause of the sensation I am having. Our concept of pain is
not "that which causes this kind of sensation" but "this kind
of sensation."

Suppose that Elwood Fritchey learns that pain is stimulated C-fibers. He already knew that pain was pain and that
the state of having stimulated C-fibers was the state of having stimulated C-fibers. The antecedent physicalist cannot
capture what he learns in terms of the subject matter content. The change in his mind will be that his concept of pain
and his concept of stimulated C-fibers become linked. The
reflexive content of his new thought captures this change:

that there is some state that is referred to by both the concept of pain and the concept of stimulated C-fibers.

If we turn things around, we get at what Elwood failed to know, the bit of ignorance that made him think it was possible that pain was not stimulated C-fibers. His pain concept and his stimulated C-fibers concept were not linked. There were ways of fitting his concepts onto the world so that they did not co-refer, and yet the conditions that his thought put on things were met. This bit of ignorance is the possibility that is eliminated by the identity.

But there is an apparent problem here. It seems that there is a very intimate, even necessary, connection between one's Humean idea of pain, and pain. That idea cannot resemble any sensations but pain sensations. And it also seems that Elwood's scientific concept of stimulated C-fibers, insofar as it is accurate and relatively detailed, will include logically necessary and sufficient conditions for being that state. If neither of Elwood's concepts *can* be fit onto any state but their actual referents, and their actual referents are one and the same, then it seems that even the reflexive content of Elwood's thought will be necessary, and the reflexive content of his condition of ignorance will be impossible. Not only is pain necessarily stimulated C-fibers, but the concepts of pain (with our Humean idea of pain at its core) and the concept of stimulated C-fibers (with essential structural properties at its core) must co-refer. But then where is the antecedent physicalist to find contingency?

Consider two of Elwood Fritchey's thoughts about pain and C-fibers:

a. While in pain, he thinks, "This$_i$ sensation is not the stimulation of C-fibers."

b. While not in pain, employing his Humean idea of pain, he thinks, "Pain is not the stimulation of C-fibers."

Case (a) is a case of failure of recognition. Elwood is attending to an inner state of which he already has a concept but does not realize it. Elwood has a concept of a certain kind of state that meets various scientific criteria determined by the body of knowledge in brain science. He does not *apply* that concept to the sensation he feels. He does not *call* it "stimulation of C-fibers." He does not suppose the sensation to have the location and structure implied by the scientific concept. Also, he does not take the sensation to be a *source* of information about the state. From the point of view of information flow, he has a buffer ("this sensation") that is of a certain state but is not attached to his concept of that state, either as applicandum or as source.

For Elwood to believe that the sensation he is having is the stimulation of C-fibers, the crucial change that has to be made in his cognitive states is a link between the buffer and the concept. The concept *already* fits the sensation; the concept and the buffer are *already* of the same state. The reflexive content that captures the additional demand that the new belief places on the world is simply that the referent of his stimulated C-fibers concept and the inner state he is in and is attending to are one and the same. There is nothing contradictory or incoherent about the content of his current state at this reflexive level, since we are abstracting from the sensation his inner attention buffer is of.

Let's now turn to case (b). The antecedent physicalist supposes that Elwood has two unlinked concepts of the same inner state: the scientific concept, which we are supposing to incorporate essential properties of the inner state to which it refers, and the demonstrative/recognitional concept with a Humean idea at its core. We are supposing this Humean idea to necessarily resemble the sensation of pain; it couldn't *fit* any other sensation.

The Humean idea at the core of the pain concept does not guarantee, however, that the source or applicandum of this concept will always be the state that it necessarily resembles. Suppose that Elwood falsely believes that pain is relaxed D-fibers. His relaxed D-fibers concept and his pain concept are linked. When he feels pain, he notes the conditions under which it occurs, and this feeds into his concept of D-fiber relaxation. He believes that if he looked through his auto-cerebroscope or had a colleague check his brain while he is in pain, relaxed D-fibers would be encountered. When he reads about ways of avoiding relaxed D-fibers, he incorporates those into his pain concept as ways of avoiding pain.

Elwood is mistaken, and his mistake involves belief in an impossibility, since stimulated C-fibers and relaxed D-fibers are two states and cannot be one. But his belief is not incoherent. A Humean idea of pain necessarily resembles a case of pain; a normal person who is applying the concept to a state he is in will apply it only to pain; a normal person who is using a state he is in as a source of information for the concept will use, among the states he might be in and attending to, only the state of pain. But the antecedent physicalist believes that there are many ways to encounter the state of pain other than by having it. One can read about an inner state and take it to be pain or not. One can see an inner state through an autocerebroscope and take it to be pain or not. One can be shrunk, like Arthur and Raquel, slog around inside some one else's brain, and take a state one sees to be the state of pain or not. In all of these cases, one may be applying the pain concept, with its Humean core, to a state that is not the state of pain, and one may be using such a state as a source of information about the state of pain. The Humean core guides our application or withholding of the concept only to states we are aware of by being in them, not to states we see, read about, and the like.

In cases like this, the various strands that make up our paradigm of reference pull apart. When Elwood gathers information about pain by having pain, or when he applies his concept to the state of pain while he is in it, the state of stimulated C-fibers is serving as the source and applicandum of his concept of pain. But when Elwood reads about relaxed D-fibers and pours information into his pain concept, information is flowing from observations about one thing into a concept of another. When he is told his D-fibers are going to be relaxed and he uses his Humean idea of pain to anticipate what he will feel, he is applying his concept of pain to relaxed D-fibers. In some circumstances stimulated C-fibers are the source and applicandum of his concept of pain, at other times, relaxed D-fibers.

So far we are imagining Elwood to resist identifying pain with stimulation of C-fibers because he has another candidate in mind. Of course, this is not the dualist's view. The dualist thinks that no identification between the state of pain and a physical state can be correct. From the antecedent physicalist's point of view, the state the dualist's idea of pain fits, the applicandum, and the source are all the same, the state of pain. But during other sorts of encounters with pain, such as reading about C-fibers and their stimulation, staring at his own stimulated C-fibers through an autocerebroscope or walking around inside the brain of a person in pain and looking at her stimulated C-fibers, he does not apply his concept or use the pain he observes as a source for adding information to it.

In either case, the information flow is blocked because the concept of pain is not linked to the concept of stimulated C-fibers. The real possibility that underlies the sense of contingency is simply the negation of the crucial fact that would have to be learned to know that pain is the stimulation of C-fibers. It is the possibility that the two concepts are unlinked, that they do not in fact co-refer.

Is it possible that these concepts do not co-refer? If we keep what's in them fixed, it may seem that they must co-refer. The scientific concept describes the state of pain by its essential neurological, chemical, and other scientific properties; the Humean idea of pain necessarily fits only the state of pain. Even with these items fixed, however, it does not follow that either of these concepts *refer* to the state of pain, and hence it does not follow that they co-refer. We must distinguish between

• worlds in which Elwood's two concepts do not co-refer, and

• worlds in which Elwood's scientific concept does not denote the same state his Humean idea fits.

Reference is not a matter of denotation or fit but of the circumstantial facts that determine source and applicandum. There are many possible ways these facts might be different. There are worlds in which scientists, perhaps because of lack of proper funding, manage to come up with a concept that denotes stimulated C-fibers but for which some other state X is both source and applicandum. This world would be strange but not impossible.

Our term "unicorn" suggests a model for this. According to the standard account, unicorns are mythical beasts. According to the account Avrom Faderman defends, our concept of a unicorn actually stems from a bad theory of ibexes.

Suppose Faderman is right about the original source of the concept. And suppose that the concept was not co-opted by mythology. It is applied to ibexes; they are hunted for the valuable single horn, even though the few that have been caught have all been (it is thought) valueless mutants with two horns. Even if there were, somewhere, animals that fit all of the criteria in the concept for being unicorns, so that the concept denoted them or fit them, the concept would be of ibexes.[25]

One might respond that Elwood and the dualist certainly do not believe in a world where scientists have a bad account of one state that happens to fit another. But we must recall that the various worlds that are used to represent what a person does *not* believe do not provide alternative things one of which the person *does* believe. The point of the indefinitely many possible worlds that fit the above description—worlds where some *other* state X is the referent of a concept that denotes stimulated C-fibers—is not that one of these involves what Elwood (or the dualist) thinks *is* going on, but that none of them includes what Elwood and the dualist do *not* think is going on.

A slightly different question is this. Why, if pain is the only state that fits our concept of pain, and pain is the only state denoted by our concept of stimulated C-fibers, should it not be *obvious* that they are the same? Or at least a priori? Why shouldn't someone who is careful and willing to spend enough time on the problem be able to figure it out?

Here, ironically, the natural appeal of the antecedent dualist is to the Ewing gap. Think how different it is to *have* a pain than to read about a brain state or examine one in any of the more or less fanciful ways we have imagined. Having a pain is *nothing at all* like seeing anything one might see through an autocerebroscope, or by being small and slog-ging around in a brain, or by looking at images from expensive microscopes. Our *phenomenological* concept of pain is not introduced, explicitly or implicitly, in terms of the concepts of brain science. The concepts of brain science are not introduced as shorthand for patterns of qualia. The relevant relation is not definability or supervenience but identity. It is just the sort of identity that one would not expect to discover a priori. And of course the antecedent physicalist does not think that it is to be discovered a priori, but by discovering through extensive empirical research that the brain state of having stimulated C-fibers plays the causal role that pain plays.

There is one way in which we might suppose such identities could be discovered (in some sense) a priori—somewhat reminiscent of Hume's missing shade of blue. Once a number of identities have been established and the various ways in which families of sensations differ from one another have been identified with scientifically described variations among families of brain states, it may be possible to predict, on the basis of what is already known, what it will be like to have some hitherto unexperienced sensation, or at least to select, from experienced sensations, the one that is scientifically described in a certain way.

The reply to Kripke, then, is that even if pain and other sensations do not fit the model of heat or water, the antecedent physicalist has a number of ways of dealing with the sense of contingency involved with the thought that pain is stimulated C-fibers. At the level of information flow, it is not difficult to see the difference between believing in this identity, withholding assent from it, or believing in some other identity. We can see what changes would constitute a change from these states to belief in the identity. We cannot find a real possibility for the thought that pain is not stimulated C-fibers at the subject matter level, as Kripke observes. But we can find real possibilities at the reflexive levels of content that give us a grip on how the mind and the world it represents might fit together in a way that makes the thought true and explain the sort of internal coherence it has, even in the face of its necessarily falsity.

8.3   Chalmers' Argument

Chalmers recognizes two levels of content. There are two propositions associated with thoughts and statements, which he calls the primary and the secondary propositions. The secondary propositions are basically subject matter contents. (It won't matter for our purposes whether we think of them as denotation-loaded or denotation-unloaded.) The primary propositions are rather like the criterial contents we introduced in discussing Krikpe. For example, with "Heat is molecular motion," the secondary proposition is necessary; rapid molecular motion is heat in all possible worlds. But the primary proposition is not: rapid molecular motion doesn't cause the sensation of heat, and so on, in all possible worlds. The primary proposition explains our sense of contingency. Primary propositions also retreat from the references of proper names and indexicals. Proper names won't be important for our discussion; the basic idea is that we have criteria for their use, and primary propositions keep those criteria relevant, rather than fixing the referent. We'll discuss Chalmers' treatment of indexicals in a bit.

   The sort of explanation that works with "Heat is molecular motion" doesn't work with "Pain is stimulated C-fibers." The explanation with heat depends on the fact that the criteria in our concept of heat don't pick out the same physical processes in every possible world. There are worlds in which something other than rapid molecular motion causes the characteristic sensation. That's why the primary proposition can be contingent. But Chalmers says our ordinary concept of pain *does* pick out the same sensation in every possible world. And the scientific concept of "stimulated C-fibers" picks out the same brain state in every possible world. So if pain is stimulated C-fibers, the primary proposition will be necessary, as well as the secondary proposition. But Chalmers says the primary proposition is clearly not necessary, so the identity must not be true.

Bearing in mind the lessons of chapter 6 and the discussion in this chapter so far, the natural place to balk is at the use of the level of primary propositions to model the thought of one who is considering the possibility of whether a given sensation is identical with a brain state. Since the identity is unreflected in the mind of the agent, the apparatus we use to model that mind must allow us to abstract from the connections between the mind of the agent and the object or property twice represented therein.

To this one might respond that the issue here is not thought but possibility. But this is not quite right. The antecedent physicalist agrees that if a brain state is a sensation it is so necessarily. The question is not how to model that. The issue is the validity of an inference, from the existence of a thought that cannot be excluded a priori and is, in some sense, internally coherent, that an identity is not true, to the conclusion that the identity is not necessary, and so in fact not true. To judge that, we need to model the premise as well as the conclusion. Before considering that, however, we need to look at an important wrinkle in Chalmers' primary propositions.

Context and Circumstance

In the last twenty-five years or so, the grip of the objective
ideal and the subject matter assumption has been broken a
bit to deal with cases involving indexicality and demonstration. To return to the Dretske case, if I had said, early in the
conversation, "You are not Fred Dretske," I would not have
expressed a real possibility. We can get at my ignorance, at
the possibility I need to eliminate, at the reflexive level, with
the property of being a speaker of the utterance who is talking to Fred Dretske at the time of the utterance. It is a contingent fact that I was then such a speaker. A number of systems provide a level that officially recognizes this possibility
and gives it some status as a backup when one encounters
the sort of mistake I made—ignorance about various sorts
of "locating knowledge." Chalmers' system of primary and
secondary propositions incorporates one way of doing this.

In Chalmers' system, handling locating knowledge is *one*
role of primary intensions that they can perform in virtue
of a complication. Primary intensions are not functions simply from worlds to extensions but from *centered* worlds to
extensions. A centered world is a world plus a center; a center consists of an agent and time. The contextual facts for
the interpretation of a statement with "I" or "now" in it are
facts about what the chosen agent is doing at the chosen
time. When I said "You are not Dretske" to Dretske, we can't
capture my ignorance with secondary intensions. We can't
find a possibility the elimination of which would solve my
problem, because there aren't any worlds in which Dretske
isn't himself. But at the level of primary intensions we find
centered worlds with me and the time of the party as chosen agent and time, talking to someone who is not Dretske.
These are the possibilities I need to eliminate.

Note that centered worlds are not new real possibilities. They are real possibilities *plus* something. Set theoretically, we have a pair of things. The world represents a way things might be, a real possibility. The chosen agent and time do not represent further information about that world; they do not represent further arrangements for the objects and properties in the world. What, then, do they do?

Consider a system with four simple possible worlds: w', in which Elwood is in California and Mary is in Ohio; w'', in which Mary is in California and Elwood is in Ohio; w''' with both in California; and w'''' with both in Ohio. For simplicity, leave times out of it, leave everyone but Elwood and Mary out of it, leave everywhere but California and Ohio out of it. A center simply consists of an agent, either Elwood or Mary. So we have a system with eight centered worlds.

Suppose Elwood wakes up in California with a case of amnesia. He doesn't remember who he is or where he is. We would characterize Elwood's state of ignorance with the set consisting of all eight centered worlds. He knows he is someone and is somewhere. That is modeled by the fact that each agent in each world is somewhere. He doesn't know who he is. That is modeled by the fact that there are different agents in the centers. He doesn't know where he is. That is modeled by the fact that the agents are in different places in the worlds. Let's look at some of the things Elwood might learn.

Case 1: He first figures out who he is, perhaps checking his driver's license. He expresses what he learns by saying "I am Elwood." What he learns is modeled by eliminating the centered worlds with Mary at the center.

Case 2: He first figures out where he is, perhaps by seeing a sign outside the motel window, "Welcome to California."

He expresses what he learns by saying "I am in California." What he learns is modeled by eliminating the worlds in which the agent lives in Ohio.

In case 1, the subject matter possibilities do not change at all. Worlds w' through w'''' remain in the primary proposition that models Elwood's knowledge. All that changes is the centers that remain: the ones with Mary at the center are eliminated.

In case 2, we eliminate the two centered worlds with w'''', where no one lives in California, and the other centered worlds in which the agent lives in Ohio.

What do these changes represent? The centers link the utterance of "I" with an individual. Centered worlds with different agents, disagreeing on which is linked to the utterance of "I," cancel each other out, in the familiar way that conflicting facts in sets of possible worlds do. By containing worlds in which a given fact obtains and other worlds in which the given fact does not obtain, a proposition leaves open the question of whether the fact obtains or not. In the same way, a primary proposition with different centers leaves open the question of who the agent is, and hence who is linked to the utterance of "I," and hence *what the subject matter of the statement or thought is.* In case 1, the change is that Elwood links his self-buffer to his Elwood notion. In case 2, he links his present-location buffer to his notion of California. The centers then are ways of representing facts about the utterance or thought being analyzed, without requiring that utterance or thought to be part of the subject matter. They are ways of getting at reflexive content.

The system of centered worlds, then, is basically a way of representing the difference between belief states that don't differ in their subject matter content but do differ in their reflexive contents. The center tells us who the relevant speaker or thinker is and when the relevant utterance or thought occurs. The center is ultimately a connection between the agents and times in the modeling worlds and the self-notion and now-buffer of the agent the content of whose thoughts or utterances are being modeled. To deal with indexical thoughts and utterances, the primary truth-conditions of thoughts and utterances are given parameters for agents and times. A primary proposition with such parameters is basically a somewhat disguised reflexive truth-condition. At the center, the reflexive truth conditions *fit onto* the world.

Why the disguise? Why not simply have the utterances and thoughts one is considering in the possible worlds with which one models their truth-conditions? I think the main explanation is historical. Possible-worlds semantics was developed to model subject matter possibilities for the purposes of logic, then adapted to the needs of epistemology. As we emphasized in chapter 6, what is loaded is not part of the subject matter. This is why it is not a (subject matter) logical consequence of the statement "I am sitting" that anyone is speaking. What the statement says (its subject matter content) could be true in a world in which no one was thinking or saying anything at the time, as long as I was sitting. By keeping the loading out of worlds or "off-stage," one avoids unwanted consequences. This was the reason for the two-level systems in Kaplan 1989 and the relational approach in *Situations and Attitudes* (Barwise and Perry 1999). This sort of streamlining seems to me somewhat misguided outside of the context of logic (and perhaps undermotivated within). The present goal, however, is not to criticize Chalmers' semantic system (which in fact has many attractive features) but to see if it really supports his neo-dualism.

Here is one way to think about what is going on. The words "I" and "now" are associated by the rules of language with *roles* people and times play with respect to utterances and thoughts, not with *properties* of people and times. The linguistic roles are being the speaker of the utterance and being the time at which the utterance takes place; the cognitive roles are being the thinker or owner of the thought, and being the time of the thought. But these roles are not part of the subject matter of the thoughts; the subject matter includes the *occupants* of the role, not the roles themselves.

"I" and "now" are not the only words that express roles and for which there is a gap between role and subject matter. The same is true with "here," to take an obvious example. In one of its senses, "here" provides the role being the place of the utterance. Suppose, then, that we have a system like Chalmers'. How should we handle "here"? One might consider adding another parameter, for places, to the centers. Alternatively, we can identify a place to occupy the role of "here" in terms of the parameters we already have: being the place of the chosen agent at the chosen time. Suppose, standing in Worms, I say "Here is where Luther stood." The first method can model this without requiring the modeling worlds to ever have me in Worms (what is loaded is no longer relevant). The second method will require them to have me in Worms, for only my being there in the world identifies Worms as the place Luther had to stand for the statement to be true. A subject matter–oriented logic will favor the first method, since it isn't a subject matter consequence of my statement that I have ever been in Worms or ever existed at all, for that matter.

In chapter 6 we saw that there was a difference between indexicality and reflexivity. In the case of indexicality the rules of language instruct users as to which contextual factors determine the reference of particular utterances. The reference of all other types of words and all sorts of ideas is also determined by which objects play which roles relative to a given utterance or thought. How do we handle reflexivity in general in Chalmers' system? We have to do with what we are given, which is quite a bit: an agent, a time, and a world with all sorts of things playing all sorts of roles vis-à-vis the agent at that time.

Consider a local variant on Putnam's elms and beeches example. During the summer I don't know how to tell apart the live oaks and the blue oaks that one finds in California's foothills. I am actually fairly knowledgeable about both kinds of trees. I know that live oaks are evergreens whereas blue oaks are deciduous, so I can tell them apart most of the year. But in the summer, they both have leaves and look a lot alike. I am looking at a famous tree, the Black Bart Tree in Copperopolis, California, under which the famous outlaw held up a Wells Fargo stage on which Bret Harte and Mark Twain were riding.[26] The tree is in fact a live oak. But I can't be sure.

When I say "that kind of tree," I refer to the kind "California live oak," but it is possible for me to think that this is not right, that the tree is a blue oak. My thought would be mistaken but not incoherent.

The problem, analyzed at an information flow level, is that I have a concept of California live oaks, a concept of blue oaks, and a buffer for the kind of tree I am looking at. But the buffer is not linked to my concept of California live oaks.

Clearly, my problem is recognition; I have a concept of California live oaks, but I don't recognize this as an instance of it. I don't think of the species California live oak as "that kind of tree." The difference recognition would bring is treated as reflexive content, that my concept of California live oaks and my buffer for the kind of tree to which I am attending co-refer. It is the difference in reflexive content that reflects the change that would occur if I went from merely knowing "that kind of tree is that kind of tree" to knowing "that kind of tree is a California live oak."

How can we represent this situation in Chalmers' system of primary and secondary intensions? We'll assume I know who I am and what day and time it is, so I am the agent, and the time I have these thoughts is the chosen time for each of our centered worlds. What do the worlds themselves have to be like?

We might consider varying the tree I am looking at, the Black Bart live oak in some worlds, a similar-looking blue oak in others. This would model the situation in which I don't know which tree I am looking at. But I do know which tree I am looking at; it is the Black Bart tree.

We might consider the centered worlds in which I'm looking at the Black Bart tree but let the worlds vary on the issue of whether it is a California live oak or a blue oak. We would be modeling the situation in which I am looking at a tree that really might be a California live oak or might be a blue oak. But (arguably) the species of a tree is an essential property of it, so the blue oak worlds are not real possibilities.

Still, these strategies seem sort of along the right lines. Although it is a necessary fact about the Black Bart tree that it is a California live oak, that necessary fact is not reflected in my concept of the Black Bart tree. It is an unreflected necessity. So we might consider having two centered worlds in each of which there is a tree I am looking at that fits all of the things I know about the Black Bart tree. The tree in one world is a California live oak; the tree in the other world is a blue oak. When I learn that the Black Bart tree is a California live oak, I eliminate the centered worlds in which the agent is looking at the blue oak Black Bart look-alike. We seem to have a strategy for representing unreflected modalities within Chalmers' system. In such a case there will be a concept of the object in question that does not include the modal fact. We have two worlds in which different objects fit the concept but in which the modal facts don't differ: the blue oaks are necessarily blue oaks and the live oaks necessarily live oaks in both worlds. The ignorance of the agent is represented by his not knowing which world he is in.

But what if the situation is like this? My concept of the Black Bart tree in fact contains a certain property Z. And property Z is necessarily connected with being a California live oak, although I don't know it. We can't use our strategy, for there will be no possible world in which a blue oak tree fits my notion of the Black Bart tree.

There will, however, be worlds in which my notion of the Black Bart tree is a notion *of* a blue oak tree. In the terminology of chapter 6, the blue oak tree will be the source and the applicandum but not a member of the denotation. In these blue oak worlds, my notion will contain a mistake, since blue oak trees don't have property Z. So my notion of the Black Bart tree contains property Z; if my notion is correct, the Black Bart tree has to be a California live oak and my belief is false; if my belief is true, my notion must be mistaken about the tree having Z.

Within Chalmers' system, then, we can model my epistemic situation with centered worlds with me as agent and the time at which my thought occurred as time, in some of which the notion I have has the Black Bart tree as source and applicandum and is accurate and incomplete, and in others of which that notion has some blue oak look-alike as source and applicandum and is not accurate, since the blue oak will not have property Z. This will be the *primary* intension of my state of ignorance. The change that occurs when I figure out that the Black Bart tree is a California live oak is that the blue oak look-alike worlds are removed.

Chalmers' system, then, potentially has considerable power and flexibility, as long as we make sure that the ideas of the agents and the various connections they might have to the world have a place in the possible worlds, so that we can avoid sliding into the subject matter assumption.[27]

It seems to me that Kripke and Chalmers have each recognized that some retreat from the subject matter assumption is required to understand the throughts about what is necessary and what is not, our sense of contingency. Kripke brings in the criteria we associate with natural-kind terms; Chalmers introduces a whole formal apparatus built around such criteria, plus a way of handling indexicality. But to extend the military metaphor, they are too courageous. They retreat from the subject matter assumption but want to set up a line fairly near that battleground. I advocate wholesale, headlong, go-for-broke retreat, explicitly recognizing all levels of content I can find, abandoning the subject matter assumption completely.[28]

Let's consider Mary from the point of an enriched Chalmersian framework. Mary's notions and ideas and their connections to things are part of what the worlds contain.

Mary doesn't know whether Q_R is B_{47} or not; she thinks it is, she has argued that it is, but she realizes the evidence is not conclusive. She stares at a red wall and hopes, "This$_i$ subjective character is B_{47}." What she is attending to is not B_{47}, but B_{52}. And we can't say that B_{47} might have caused that sensation, because it isn't *causing* that is at issue, it's *being*. That sensation *is* B_{52}.

From an information flow point of view, her ignorance consists in not having her "the sensation I am attending to" buffer linked to her concept of B_{52} and not having the Humean idea of her current impression in her concept of B_{52}, and so not having the properties of being Q_R and being called "Q_R" in her concept of B_{52}. She does not have the ability to tell the difference between B_{52} and B_{47} by being in them and attending to them.

Within the reflexive-referential account, we can say that the reflexive content of her belief (or hope) that Q_R is B_{47} is that her Q_R concept, including her Humean idea of the sensation of red, and her concept of brain state B_{47} co-refer. Since they do not in fact co-refer, this can only be true if one or the other or both do not refer to the things they actually refer to. Given that both concepts contain ideas that fit their references essentially, this can only happen if one or other concept or both does not fit the object to which it refers.

What of the Chalmersian primary intension? We can model her hope with worlds in which her concept of B_{47} is the concept *of* the very sensation she is having: that type of sensation is the source and applicandum of the concept. In some of these worlds, her concept of B_{47} will have the sensation seeing red as source and applicandum; in these worlds the concept will be incorrect, for its referent does not have the properties required of it by the concept. In others, her concept of Q_R will be a concept of the sensation one has when one sees puce—a sensation I'll call "Q_P." It will not fit that sensation; the Humean idea will not fit the sensation to which it is applied; the concept will have as a source and applicandum a sensation that does not fit the Humean ideas that it incorporates. That is, in the worlds in which the primary proposition is true, one or the other of the concepts involved will be somewhat pathological in not denoting the state they are of. But such worlds, however odd, are possible and provide the real possibility that underlies Mary's hope. Given the necessary identities that Q_R *is* B_{52}, and that Q_P *is* B_{47}, how can the belief she has in virtue of the link between her Q_R concept and her B_{47} concept be true? Only by her Q_R

concept being of Q_P, or by her B_{47} concept being of B_{52}. If her concepts are of what they denote, her belief will be false. If her belief is true, her concepts will not denote what they are of.

The Autocerebroscope

Another large surprise awaits Mary in what I'll call "the Feigl room": the autocerebroscope (Feigl 1967, 14, 14n). With this Mary can simultaneously have a sensation and observe it in her own brain. Feigl imagined this on analogy with a fluoroscope, so that Mary would be looking at something like a pattern on a monitor of her brain activity. With our more up to date imaginations, we can imagine it attached to some sort of electron microscope that can be aimed right at the location or locations in her brain relevant to her subjective character, or at least to the places where activity would differ depending on whether B_{52} or B_{47} were occurring. B_{47}, she is told, is actually the subjective character associated with seeing puce objects. She learns quickly how to use the scope. She watches (with her right eye) what happens in her own brain as she shifts her look (with her left eye) from a red surface to a puce surface. There is no doubt about it. She was wrong.

Still, she could have the following thought (using "$this_{ac}$" for her attention to the autocerebroscope):

$This_{ac}$ brain state (left eye on puce surface) might have been $this_i$ subjective character (left eye on red surface). I might have been right.

On the "$this_i$ subjective character" side of the identity, there are the same lines of semantic retreat as before. We can retreat to "the subjective character to which the agent is attending at the time." On the other side, the autocerebroscope provides Mary with as direct a perception of a brain as we can imagine, almost as good as being inside Leibniz's mill-size brain or in the boat with the tiny scientists of *Fantastic Voyage*. That is still not as direct, however, as *being in* a brain state. There is a criteria/reference distinction to be made when it comes to looking at a brain state, even if it is your own. Mary could consistently imagine looking at the red surface with her left eye and having Q_R while looking in the autocerebroscope with her right eye and having the experiences she in fact has only when she looks at the *puce* surface with her left eye. If we abstract from the reference of the autocerebroscope pattern to the brain state B_{47}, while retaining its association with the name "B_{47}" as it appears in Mary's thinking (and publications), we get roughly the proposition that Q_R appears like so and so on an autocerebroscope, and meets the various scientific criteria for being called "B_{47}," and is what Mary was referring to in her journal articles. That's the coherent content of Mary's hope and imagination, the coherent basis that provides an illusion of contingency for the awful necessary truth that Q_R is really B_{52}, her conjecture wrong, her career shattered, and probably a long career in minor administrative posts the most she can hope for.

I think, then, that there are enough contingencies, discoverable by using the content analyzer as we semantically retreat from one or the other of the terms in the various necessary identities we have considered, to explain Mary's various feelings of contingency in the face of them. Since these contingencies are there, we can find them in any reasonable system for representing the contents of statement and thought, including Chalmers'.

I want to end this discussion with a brief disclaimer, however. A number of problems plague attempts to use possible-worlds semantics to model knowledge and belief, not all of

which reduce to the subject matter fallacy. All the suggestions I have given about representing Mary's or Elwood's
beliefs will be susceptible to these problems, which have
nothing to do with dualism but are simply artifacts of this
approach to epistemology. For example, because of the complete nature of possible worlds and the structure of the usual
analyses of knowledge and belief, a believer is implausibly
taken to believe everything entailed by her beliefs. Some of
these problems can be addressed by using situations or some
other partial way of representing worlds. I'm not going into
these topics in this book (see, however, Barwise and Perry
1999; Perry 1986a, 1989).

8.4   Ewing's Intuition

As philosophy books go, this one is not so long. But perhaps
it is too long, given the simplicity of the message. The antecedent physicalists and the neo-dualists agree that being
aware of our own experiences is much different than reading about or perceiving brain states in any way imagined
in philosophy or film. There are clearly two quite different
epistemic phenomena, two ways of knowing, two kinds of
awareness, two practices of analysis and description, two
different vocabularies. The question is whether that means
that there are two things known about. The neo-dualist
says "yes" in various ways with various arguments; the antecedent physicalist says "no" in various ways with various
rebuttals.

   This back and forth extends the pattern of the history of
the mind-body problem since Descartes. It has been (among
other things) the consistent advance of physicalistic monism
over various forms of dualism, with new forms of the latter rising from the ashes of the older forms at each stage.

Each new version articulates the thought that surely *some-thing* more is going on with us than the merely physical. In Cartesian dualism, the mind is one thing, the brain another. The essence of the mind is thought or consciousness, the essence of material things is extension. No matter how hard you think or how vividly you imagine, you don't get extension out of it; no matter how you pound and flatten and shape something extended, you don't get a thought. There is simply no way of being physical that adds up to being mental or vice versa: the experience gap argument raised to a basic principle of metaphysics. Then Spinoza asked why there could not be a single thing that had both of these fundamental properties, a sort of metaphysical substance that, like the Dalai Lama, instantiates two very different but not incompatible sets of properties. As Stuart Hampshire has observed, Spinoza was in a sense the first identity theorist.

The result of this insight was not the death of dualism but a new weaker form, property-dualism. Locke, for another example, admits that for all he knows spiritual substance and material substance are the same and that God has enabled matter to think (Locke 1694: bk. IV, chap. 3). He conceived of thought as something God would have to add to the usual properties of matter.[29] Mental properties are properties of the brain or of the physical person; they are not, however, physical properties of the brain or person, but a different kind of property. There is *something else* going on, even if the subject of these goings-on is a physical object of one sort or another.

In our own era, the identity theory was reborn in Feigl's seminal essay, from which I have gleaned the quotations at beginnings of the chapters (Feigl 1967). Feigl's essay as well as articles that followed by U. T. Place (1956) and J. J. C. Smart (1959) incorporated ideas and distinctions from philosophy of language and brought the old debate into analytical philosophy. In his article, Smart showed that many arguments against identifying brain states and mental states failed once one took account of intensionality, intentionality, and other important phenomena that make it difficult to prove a nonidentity.

The experience gap argument still posed a problem, however. It presents us with an experience of our own, of which we are aware in the way we are usually aware of our own experiences, and a brain event, known, or at least imagined to be known, in some quite different way, perhaps through Feigl's autocerebroscope. The properties we are aware of are not ones we observe the brain event to have. But does it follow that it does not have those properties, that the very event we observe isn't the one that we feel as intense and unpleasant? Perhaps there is simply one set of properties of the event available to feeling and another, quite different set available through perception? This claim is surely open to the identity theorist. There is just one brain event, known in two quite different ways, via some form of physical perception or description of brain states and via first-person awareness. A single state or event has all the properties disclosed to each via each method.

But then is the identity theorist really a physicalist? Or a double-aspect theorist, a property dualist of brains or brain events?

This question, as posed by Max Black, gave Smart the most trouble (Smart 1959). And with his question, Black forged a link between the philosophy of mind and Frege's problem and gave the philosophy of mind a semantical turn. What makes the identity informative? Even if an experience is admitted to be a brain state, must one not admit that whatever property the brain state has that makes it *also* an experience and provides the surprise is nonphysical?

Smart's strategy was to appeal to topic-neutral concepts of physical properties. The prevailing application of that strategy has been to find this neutrality in causal-role or functional properties that a brain state might have. I have argued that this version of the topic-neutral strategy is a mistake when applied to the phenomenal side of mind, to subjective characters, qualia, raw feels, that is, to experience. We need instead the topic-neutrality of demonstrative/recognitional concepts.

We can now, by way of review, see how Black's dilemma is to be avoided. Let's return to our imagined physicalist discovery, as thought by Mary, attending to her sensation of a red tomato:

This$_i$ sensation is brain state B_{52}.

This is an informative identity; it involves two modes of presentation. One is the scientifically expressed property of being B_{52}, with whatever structural, locational, compositional, and other scientific properties are encoded in the scientific term. This is not a neutral concept. The other is being a sensation that is attended to by Mary. This is a neutral concept; if the identity is true, it is a neutral concept of a physical property. Thus, according to the antecedent physicalist, Mary knows the brain state in two ways, as the scientifically described state and as the state that is playing a certain role in her life, the one she is having and to which she is attending. The state has the properties that make it mental: there is something it is like to be in it and one can attend to it in that special way we have of attending to our own inner states.

In the first chapter we considered, as a possible model for the identity theorist, the problem Molyneaux posed to Locke: whether a blind man, suddenly gaining sight, could tell, prior to any experience of correlation, what it was like to see the various shapes he knew already by touch. His cautious conjecture, and Berkeley's confident assertion, was that such a blind man would not be able to tell. The intuition is that in this case, there is identity of properties,

This$_{seen}$ shape is this$_{felt}$ shape,

which cannot be figured out a priori.

But as we noted in the first chapter, if we press this analogy, it leads toward the double-aspect theory. In this case, there are two aspects; the shape is the same, but the sensations are different.

The analogy between the antecedent physicalists' claim and the Molyneaux problem is that we have in both cases true, surprising identities that could not be determined a priori. We have two quite different ways of knowing but a single thing known. The disanalogy that the antecedent physicalist sees in the case of

This$_{ac}$ brain state is this$_i$ sensation

is that the brain state that is known by inner attention is not known by *causing* a sensation, but by *being* one. We can be aware of our sensation because we have it; we are aware of it by attending to it. No intermediary sensation is required.

The antecedent physicalist sees the neo-dualist as smuggling in an extra entity at this point; the sensation is taken as something causally downstream from the brain state; it is this nonphysical sensation, not the brain state, that is supposedly directly known. The dualists and the antecedent physicalist agree that there is a "twoness," a duality, to be explained. The antecedent physicalist insists that the two ways of knowing do not imply two things known about. The twoness does not occur in the subject matter, but in the way of knowing.

The dualists' objectionable move is then mirrored, in post-Black neo-dualist arguments, by what I have called the subject matter fallacy. In general identities can be informative because there are two ways of knowing, two modes of presentation. If modes of presentation are limited to attributive conditions of reference, then the situation cries out for another property to explain the informativeness of the identity: the Black property.

My solution has been to explain the twoness, in its various forms, not at the level of what is known about, but at the level of what is involved in the knowing: the level of reflexive content. The change in Mary, when she emerges from the Jackson room and sees the tomato, is new knowledge, because her epistemic states change in ways that change their content. The change in content cannot be reflected in new demands on the subject matter, as the physicalist conceived it, but only in new ways in which her mind makes the old demands. There is a change in reflexive content, but not in subject matter content.

The possibilities that Ewing and Chalmers and Kripke, and Mary as I imagine her, and anyone else, for that matter, envisage are not, on my analysis, possibilities that mirror the various relations the subject matters of our thoughts might have to one another but various possible ways our thoughts might fit onto the world; possibilities to be cashed out, that is, at the level of reflexive content.

If the antecedent physicalist is correct, the Chalmers zombie world is not really possible. One who knows the Chalmers zombie world is possible, then, is correct to infer that the antecedent physicalist is wrong. But how can one know this? The relevant subject matter possibility cannot be found, even using Chalmers' own system of primary and secondary intensions, unless one begins by begging the question at issue and populating the world with a layer of sensations causally downstream from brain states.

My modest conclusion, then, is that neo-dualism has not made its case. There are no doubt many obscurities and potential mysteries and problems in the antecedent physicalist view I sketched in chapters 2 and 3. But no case for incoherence or patent inadequacy, in the face of the Ewing intuition or any of its sophisticated modern variations, has been made.

Notes

1. See Block, Flanagan, and Güzeldere 1997, section 9, for some of the key papers and citations of others.

2. This concept derives ultimately from *Situations and Attitudes* (Barwise and Perry 1999), in particular the relational account of meaning and the "fallacy of misplaced information," and more recently from work with David Israel on information (see Israel and Perry 1990, 1991; Perry and Israel 1991), with Mark Crimmins on belief-attribution (Crimmins and Perry 1989) and work on the philosophy of mind and language (Perry 1993, 1977, 1979, 1990, 1997b, 1997c, 2001).

3. Chewing on zinc-coated nails is usually, perhaps always, an accident. One gets into the habit of storing a supply of nails in one's mouth while working and then becomes involved in a project that uses roofing nails, which are often zinc-coated, and unthinkingly pops some into one's mouth.

4. I'm not claiming this to really be a Latin term, merely to sound as if it ought to be Latin for "thing to which something is applied."

5. One might argue that if conscious events are physical they must have *some* physical effects, if not as a matter of logic, then as a matter of very basic physical principles. I do not think this should affect the main point I'm trying to make about Chalmers' argument. At least an unreflective physicalist might be an epiphenomenalist; such a physicalist could fit in the upper left entry of table 4.1, even if his views are ultimately not quite coherent.

6. One might argue that valves are pretty important, because one thing valves have in common is a certain role in the lives of beings with minds. Perhaps then there being valves implies the existence of things with minds.

So if minds are nonphysical, valves imply dualism. But then we might as well think about minds directly and not take a detour through valves. To return to the theological point of view, if minds are physical, then God didn't have to work on Friday to decide which objects get to be valves. If minds are not physical, then as long as he spends Friday deciding what minds are like, valves will be taken care of.

7. See Shoemaker 1997 for the history of the argument as well as an extremely subtle analysis of its use against functionalism. At the end of his postscript, Shoemaker arrives at the conclusion that one can maintain a version of functionalism in the face of the inverted spectrum argument only by giving up a bit of common sense: that it makes sense to ask if your color experiences and mine are qualitatively the same. He opts to stick with functionalism and abandon that bit of common sense where I would make the opposite choice.

8. This means that Mary must not have red hair and must not have cut herself, etc.—but exactly how Jackson guarantees that is not our problem.

9. The experiment might put her at risk on this score; perhaps some parts of her color vision system would atrophy from disuse. This is probably not the biggest problem a human subjects committee would have with this experiment.

10. Smart says that Black suggested the objection, not that he made it. Black was a connoisseur of logical and philosophical arguments in many areas in which he didn't himself hold a fixed position.

11. The Pacific APA is usually held in the San Francisco Bay area every other year and usually meets at the Claremont Hotel. A good time is had by all.

12. For a study of the semantics of paper clips, see Israel and Perry 1990.

13. See Nida-Rümelin 1995. Nida-Rümelin's room for her character Mariana is actually a whole house where the interior decoration includes only randomly colored artificial objects (no leaves or sunflowers or apples or tomatoes allowed).

14. Elwood picks up an interest in such matters by chapter 8.

15. See Evans 1973 for the concept of source and dominant source.

16. Donnellan calls the first content "attributive" and the second "referential." This terminology doesn't fit very well with mine. I try to use "reference" for indexicals and names and "denotation" for descriptions and

description-like phrases. I use "designates" and "stands for" as generic semantical relations.

17. I do not claim that the analyses of demonstratives and names incorporated into these examples are particularly sophisticated, only that they are plausible enough to make the point.

18. I often say "the reflexive content" when it would be more accurate to say "a reflexive content," since there are many reflexive contents, corresponding to the many ways one can load some facts and leave others unloaded.

19. For a more fine-grained analysis, see Perry and Israel 1991.

20. Especially in the idea that "narrow content," in Fodor's sense (Fodor 1981), should amount to what I am calling "attributive subject matter content."

21. For safety's sake, one might want to include something about braking techniques, too, but I'll ignore that here.

22. See (http://www.aiki.com) for information on this (and other) aikido moves.

23. See Perry 1989, 1986a, and 1994 for discussion of these issues.

24. Of course, it is not so easy to figure our how to do this, just as it is not easy to figure out how the phone company could add something to the phone book that would solve Terry's problem. Here are the seeds for a positive argument that dualism, in some of its forms at least, is incoherent. But in this book I am confining myself to replying to the neo-dualist arguments.

25. This is not Faderman's conclusion; see his Faderman 1997. I have also made it sound as if Faderman is fully committed to the ibex account, whereas his point is simply that it is a candidate with interesting philosophical implications.

26. Black Bart, Mark Twain, Bret Harte, Wells Fargo, Copperopolis, blue oaks, and California live oaks are all real, but the incident and the tree I made up.

27. The main problem with the system seems to me to be the obscurity that remains about what primary propositions are. As Ed Zalta has pointed out, it doesn't help to say that the primary intension of "water" is "so and so" as long as "so and so" is also something that has both a secondary and primary intension. For problems with this kind of semantical approach and related issues, see Block and Stalnaker 1999. In this chapter, however, I am

trying to locate the sense of contingency the experience gap induces in us within Chalmers' semantic system, as I understand it, without adopting his dualism.

28. Such headlong retreat must be distinguished from the position that claims that the tools of thought and devices of language are in fact themselves the subject matter of thought and language. The confusion mentioned in chapter 6, of those who confound the theory of reflexive contents with the claim that everything is really metalinguistic, is an instance of this. I do not claim that we are thinking about our own ideas or talking about our own words. Arriving at this position would be like getting turned around while in retreat and backing across enemy lines.

29. This drew upon Locke the criticism from Thomas Dodwell and others that he thought the soul was only contingently rather than necessarily immortal, which in turn provoked the important debate between Anthony Collins (who attacked Dodwell and defended Locke) and Samuel Clarke (who attacked Locke and defended Dodwell). Many of the issues currently alive in the philosophy of consciousness are discussed insightfully, albeit from a somewhat different perspective, in these letters (Clarke and Collins 1711ff).

References

Almog, Joseph, John Perry, and Howard Wettstein, eds. 1989. *Themes from Kaplan*. New York: Oxford University Press.

Barwise, Jon, and John Perry. 1999. *Situations and Attitudes*. Stanford: CSLI Publications, 1999; reprint, with additions, of Jon Barwise and John Perry, *Situations and Attitudes*. Cambridge: Bradford-MIT, 1983.

Block, Ned, Owen Flanagan, and Güven Güzeldere, eds. 1997. *The Nature of Consciousness*. Cambridge: Bradford-MIT. (Page references are to reprints in this anthology whenever possible.)

Block, Ned. 1990. Inverted Earth. In James Tomberlin, ed., *Philosophical Perspectives*, 4: 52–79. Reprinted in Block, Flanagan, and Güzeldere 1997: 478–693.

Block, Ned. 1995a. On a Confusion about a Function of Consciousness. *Behavioral and Brain Sciences*, 18: 227–247; reprinted in Block, Flanagan, and Güzeldere 1997: 375–415.

Block, Ned. 1995b. Mental Paint and Mental Latex. In Villanueva 1995.

Block, Ned. Mental Paint. In Hahn and Ramberg forthcoming.

Block, Ned, and Robert Stalnaker. 1999. Conceptual Analysis, Dualism, and the Explanatory Gap. *The Philosophical Review* 108: 1–46.

Burks, Arthur. 1949. Icon, Index and Symbol. *Philosophical and Phenomenological Research* 9: 673–689.

Chalmers, David. 1996. *The Conscious Mind*. New York: Oxford University Press.

Chalmers, David. 1999. Precis of *The Conscious Mind*. *Philosophy and Phenomenological Research* 14: 435–438.

Churchland, Paul. 1985. Reduction, Qualia, and the Direct Introspection of Brain States. *Journal of Philosophy* 82: 8–28.

Churchland, Paul. 1989. Knowing Qualia: A Reply to Jackson. Chapter 4 of Paul Churchland. *A Neurocomputational Perspective*. Cambridge: Bradford-MIT: 67–76. Reprinted in Block, Flanagan, and Güzeldere 1997: 571–577.

Clarke, Samuel, and Anthony Collins. 1711ff. *The Clarke-Collins Controversy*. (This appeared in several editions throughout the 1700s and can be found in some research libraries.)

Crimmins, Mark, and John Perry. 1989. The Prince and the Phone Booth: Reporting Puzzling Beliefs. *Journal of Philosophy* 86: 685–711. Reprinted in Perry 1993.

Davies, M., and G. Humphrey. 1993. *Consciousness*. Oxford: Blackwell.

Dennett, Daniel C. 1988. Quining Qualia. In A. Marcel and E. Bisiach, eds., *Consciousness in Contemporary Science*. Oxford: Oxford University Press: 43–77. Reprinted in Block, Flanagan, and Güzeldere 1997: 619–642.

Evans, Gareth. 1973. The Causal Theory of Names. Aristotelian Society, Supplementary Volume 47: 187–208.

Ewing, A. C. 1962. *The Fundamental Questions of Philosophy*. Paperback edition. New York: Collier Books.

Faderman, Avrom I. 1997. *Thinking, Meaning, and Speaking: Conceptual Role Semantics Reconsidered*. Ph.D. diss., Philosophy Department, Stanford University, Stanford, Calif.

Farrell, B. 1950. Experience. *Mind* 59: 170–198.

Feigl, Herbert. 1967. *The "Mental" and The "Physical": The Essay and a Postscript*. Minneapolis: University of Minnesota Press. Reprinted, with added postscript, from Herbert Feigl, Michael Scriven, and Grover Maxwell, *Minnesota Studies in the Philosophy of Science*, vol. 2. Minneapolis: University of Minnesota Press, 1958.

Fleischer, Richard, Director. 1966. *Fantastic Voyage*. 20th Century Fox. New York: CBS/Fox Video, 1990.

Fodor, Jerry. 1981. *Representations*. Brighton: Harvester Press.

Frege, Gottlob. 1892. Über Sinn und Bedeutung. *Zeitschrift für Philosophie und Philosophische Kritik*, NF 100: 25–50. Reprinted in Gottlob Frege, *Funktion, Begriff, Bedeutung: Funf logische Studien*. Edited by Günther Patzig. Göttingen: Vandenhueck & Ruprecht, 1980: 40–65.

Frege, Gottlob. 1960. On Sense and Reference. Translation of Frege 1892. In *Translations from the Philosophical Writings of Gottlob Frege*. Edited and translated by Peter Geach and Max Black. Oxford: Basil Blackwell: 56–78.

Goldman, Alvin. 1970. *A Theory of Human Action*. Englewood Cliffs, N.J.: Prentice Hall.

Hahn, Martin, and Bjorn Ramberg. Forthcoming *Others on Burge*. Cambridge: MIT.

Hilbert, David R. 1999. *Color and Color Perception: A Study in Anthropomorphic Realism*, 2nd ed. Stanford, Calif.: Center for the Study of Language and Information.

Hume, David. 1739–1740. *Treatise of Human Nature*. London.

Hume, David. 1779. *Dialogues on Natural Religion*. London.

Israel, David, and John Perry. 1990. What Is Information? In Philip Hanson, ed., *Information, Language and Cognition*. Vancouver: University of British Columbia Press: 1–19.

Israel, David, and John Perry. 1991. Information and Architecture. In Jon Barwise, Jean Mark Gawron, Gordon Plotkin, and Syun Tutiya, eds., *Situation Theory and Its Applications*, vol. 2. Stanford, Calif.: Center for the Study of Language and Information: 147–160.

Israel, David, John Perry, and Syun Tutiya. 1993. Executions, Motivations and Accomplishments. *Philosophical Review* 102: 515–540.

Jackson, Frank. 1997. What Mary Didn't Know. What Mary Didn't Know. *Journal of Philosophy* 83 (1986): 291–295. Reprinted in Block, Flanagan, and Güzeldere 1997: 567–570.

Kaplan, David. 1989. Demonstratives. In Almog 1989: 481–563.

Kripke, Saul. 1980. *Naming and Necessity*. Cambridge: Harvard University Press.

Kripke, Saul. 1997. The Identity Thesis. Excerpted from Lecture III of Kripke 1980: 144–155. In Block, Flanagan, and Güzeldere 1997: 445–450.

Künne, Wofgang, Martin Anduschus, and Albert Newen, eds. 1997. *Direct Reference, Indexicality and Propositional Attitudes*. Stanford, Calif.: Center for the Study of Language and Information–Cambridge University Press.

Leibniz, Gottfried. Written in 1714, published posthumously in 1720, n.p. *Monadology.*

Lewis, David. 1966. An Argument for the Identity Theory. *Journal of Philosophy* 63: 17–25.

Lewis, David. 1990. What Experience Teaches. In Lycan 1990: 499–519. Reprinted in Block, Flanagan, and Güzeldere 1997: 579–595.

Loar, Brian. 1990. Phenomenal States. *Philosophical Perspectives* 4: 81–108. Revised version in Block, Flanagan, and Güzeldere 1997: 597–616.

Locke, John. 1694. *Essay on Human Understanding*. 2nd ed. London.

Lycan, William G. 1990. *Mind and Cognition*. Oxford: Blackwell.

Lycan, William G. 1995. A Limited Defense of Phenomenal Information. In Metzinger 1995: 243–258.

Marcus, Ruth Barcan. 1946. A Functional Calculus of the First Order Based on Strict Implication. *Journal of Symbolic Logic* 11: 1–16.

Marcus, Ruth Barcan. 1961. Modalities and Intensional Languages. *Synthese* 13: 303–322.

McTaggart, John McTaggart Ellis. 1921, 1927. *The Nature of Existence*, vols. 1, 2. Cambridge: Cambridge University Press.

Metzinger, Thomas, ed. 1995. *Conscious Experience*. Paderborn, Germany: Frederick Schöningh.

Nagel, Thomas. 1974. What Is It Like to Be a Bat? *Philosophical Review* 83: 435–450. Reprinted in Block, Flanagan, and Güzeldere 1997: 519–527.

Nemirow, Laurence. 1979. *Functionalism and the Subjective Quality of Experience*. Ph.D. diss., Stanford University, Stanford, Calif.

Nemirow, Laurence. 1980. Review of Thomas Nagel's *Mortal Questions*. *Philosophical Review* 89: 475–476.

Nemirow, Laurence. 1989. Physicalism and the Cognitive Role of Acquaintance. In W. G. Lycan, ed., *Mind and Cognition: A Reader*. Oxford: Basil Blackwell: 490–499.

Nida-Rümelin, Martine. 1995. What Mary Couldn't Know: Belief about Phenomenal States. In Metzinger 1995: 219–241.

Nida-Rümelin, Martine. 1997. The Character of Color Predicates: A Phenomenalist View. In Künne, Anduschus, and Newen 1997: 381–402.

Perry, John. 1977. Frege on Demonstratives. *Philosophical Review* 86: 474–497. Reprinted in Perry 1993: 3–32.

Perry, John. 1979. "The Problem of the Essential Indexical." *Nous* 13: 3–21. Reprinted in Perry 1993: 33–52.

Perry, John. 1986a. From Worlds to Situations. *Journal of Philosophical Logic* 15: 83–107. Reprinted in Perry 1993: 151–171.

Perry, John. 1986b. Thought without Representation. *Supplementary Proceedings of the Aristotelian Society* 60: 263–283. Reprinted in Perry 1993: 205–225.

Perry, John. 1989. Possible Worlds and Subject Matter. In Sture Allén, ed., *Possible Worlds in Humanities, Arts and Sciences: Proceedings of the 1986 Nobel Symposium*. Berlin/New York: Walter de Gruyter: 124–138. Reprinted in Perry 1993: 173–191.

Perry, John. 1990. Self-Notions. *Logos* 11: 17–31.

Perry, John. 1993. *The Problem of the Essential Indexical*. New York: Oxford University Press.

Perry, John. 1994. Evading the Slingshot. In Andy Clark, Jesus Ezquerro, and Jesus M. Larrazabal, *Philosophy and Cognitive Science: Categories, Con sciousness, and Reasoning: Proceedings of the Second International Colloquium on Cognitive Science* Dordrecht: Kluwer Publishing. Reprinted in Perry 2000.

Perry, John. 1997a. Indexicals and Demonstratives. In Robert Hale and Crispin Wright, eds., *Companion to the Philosophy of Language*. Oxford: Blackwell: 586–612.

Perry, John. 1997b. Reflexivity, Indexicality and Names. In Künne, Anduschus, and Newen 1997: 3–19.

Perry, John. 1997c. Rip Van Winkle and Other Characters. *European Review of Philosophy* 2: 13–40. Reprinted in Perry 2000.

Perry, John. 1998. Myself and I. In Marcelo Stamm, ed., *Philosophie in Synthetisher Absicht (A Festschrift for Dieter Heinrich)*. Stuttgart: Klett-Cotta: 83–103.

Perry, John. 1999. *Dialogue on Good, Evil and the Existence of God*. Indianapolis: Hackett.

Perry, John. 2000. *The Problem of the Essential Indexical*, enlarged ed. Stanford, Calif.: Center for the Study of Language and Information–Cambridge University Press.

Perry, John. 2001. *Reference and Reflexivity*. Stanford, Calif.: Center for the Study and Language and Information.

Perry, John, and David Israel. 1991. Fodor on Psychological Explanations. In Barry Loewer and Georges Rey, eds., *Meaning in Mind*. Oxford: Basil Blackwell: 165–180. Reprinted in Perry 1993: 301–321.

Place, U. T. 1956. Is Consciousness a Brain Process? *British Journal of Psychology* 47, no. 1: 44–50.

Reichenbach, Hans. 1947. Token-reflexive words. In *Elements of Symbolic Logic*. New York: Free Press: 284–287.

Shoemaker, Sydney. 1997. The Inverted Spectrum. In Block, Flanagan, and Güzeldere 1997: 643–662.

Smart, J. J. C. 1959. Sensations and Brain Processes. *Philosophical Review* 68: 141–156.

Villanueva, E. 1995. *Philosophical Issues*. Atascadero, Calif.: Ridgeview.

Wettstein, Howard. 1981. Demonstrative Reference and Definite Descriptions. *Philosophical Studies* 40: 241–257.

Index